CRIME On eBay

Protect yourself from the dark side of eBay and PayPal.

This book should be required reading before anyone uses eBay!

You need to know how to spot fraudulent auctions. Almost all fraud on eBay results from buyers not knowing how to spot the most obvious scams. Everyone *thinks* they can spot a scam, then, two seconds later you get scammed!

You do not know what to look for even when the signs are clear, not until it is too late. Don't be a victim! You are holding in your hand the one tool that could save you from losing money, possibly having your identity stolen, and maybe even from having professional scammers clean out your bank account before you know what happened. All of these have and do happen every day to unwary and uninformed eBay users, just like you.

The sad part is it can be avoided if you just knew what was in this book....

Turn the page and see what they do not know and what you never imagined was true.

Get more information on using eBay at
DontBidOnIt.com

Trademarks

Don't Bid On It®, Snipe-To-Win®, and related names are trademarks of Elite Minds Inc. These trademarks may not be used without written permission from Elite Minds Inc. All other trademarks are the property of their respective owners whether designated as trademarks or not.

NEITHER THE PUBLISHER NOR AUTHOR MAKE ANY REPRESENTATIONS OR WARRANTIES WITH RESPECT TO THE ACCURACY OR COMPLETENESS OF THE CONTENTS OF THIS WORK AND SPECIFICALLY DISCLAIM ALL WARRANTIES, INCLUDING WITHOUT LIMITATION WARRANTIES OF FITNESS FOR A PARTICULAR PURPOSE. NO WARRANTY MAY BE CREATED OR EXTENDED BY SALES OR PROMOTIONAL MATERIALS. THE ADVICE AND STRATEGIES IN THIS WORK MAY NOT BE APPROPRIATE OR SUITABLE FOR EVERY SITUATION. THIS WORK IS SOLD WITH THE UNDERSTANDING THAT NEITHER THE PUBLISHER NOR THE AUTHOR ARE ENGAGED IN RENDERING LEGAL, ACCOUNTING, OR OTHER PROFESSIONAL SERVICES. IF PROFESSIONAL ASSISTANCE IS REQUIRED, THE SERVICES OF A COMPETENT PROFESSIONAL PERSON SHOULD BE SOUGHT. NEITHER THE PUBLISHER NOR THE AUTHOR SHALL BE LIABLE FOR DAMAGES ARISING FROM THE USE OF INFORMATION OR ADVICE IN THIS WORK. THE LISTING OF A WEBSITE, GROUP, OR ORGANIZATION IN THIS WORK DOES NOT CONSTITUTE ENDORSEMENT BY THE PUBLISHER OR AUTHOR. INTERNET WEBSITES LISTED IN THIS WORK MAY HAVE CHANGED OR DISAPPEARED SINCE THIS WORK WAS PUBLISHED.

EVERY REASONABLE ATTEMPT HAS BEEN MADE TO VERIFY THE ACCURACY OF THE INFORMATION IN THIS PROGRAM, HOWEVER NEITHER THE AUTHOR, PUBLISHER, NOR ANYONE ASSOCIATED WITH THE PRODUCTION OF THIS WORK ASSUMES ANY RESPONSIBILITY FOR ERRORS, INACCURACIES, OR OMISSIONS. THIS PROGRAM MAY MAKE SUGGESTIONS REGARDING MARKETING, SALES, AND ADVERTISING, WHICH ARE GOVERNED BY STATE LAWS WHICH MAY VARY. CHECK YOUR LOCAL LAWS AND THE RULES AND REGULATIONS OF EBAY. THE EBAY RULES AND REGULATIONS MAY HAVE CHANGED SINCE THIS PROGRAM WAS CREATED. SOME EBAY FEATURES REFERENCED IN THIS PROGRAM MAY HAVE CHANGED OR BEEN REMOVED SINCE THIS PROGRAM WAS PRODUCED.

For copyright reasons, all auctions shown in this program are either created by the author or are simulated auction pages created for the purposes of illustration. The user ID's are fictitious or obscured to maintain the privacy of eBay users. All images were created for this program or are known to be royalty free or public domain images, or were used with permission of the copyright holder.

eBay® is a trademark of eBay Inc. PayPal® is a registered trademark of PayPal Inc. This program was produced independently by Elite Minds Incorporated and is not a product of or endorsed by eBay Inc. or PayPal Inc.

Crime On eBay
Previously published as Scams and Scoundrels First Edition
Published by Elite Minds Inc, 355 N Lantana St #562, Camarillo CA 93010

ISBN 0-9845361-0-8
ISBN-13 978-0-9845361-0-8
©2007-2012 Elite Minds Inc., All Rights Reserved.

For more information, bulk quantities, and other books, visit
www.EliteMindsInc.com or www.ScamsAndScoundrels.com

ABOUT THE AUTHOR

Michael Ford began his eBay career in 1998 and first became a power seller in 2001. His business has since expanded beyond eBay, but he still enjoys buying and selling on eBay as a collector of antique arcade games. Michael has authored a number of books including *Practical PC Security* and *Ebay 102*, which explains eBay auctions and members as they have never been revealed. He is a regular contributor to collector magazines and he is a well known business writer.

Michael has always been an entrepreneur and eBay has developed those independent business drives into several full-fledged commercial ventures.

Michael is known for **telling it like it is** and has a no nonsense approach to business and writing. Michael's amateur psychologist side also led him to monitor the unsavory side of eBay which resulted in protection measures that are commonly used to identify fraudulent buyers and sellers.

Michael knows both the good and bad sides of eBay and has shared his experiences and techniques to help members gain the most from eBay without losing their shirt to scammers.

QUICK REFERENCE

Scam Check for Buyers

- Beware of sellers with only buying feedback history or zero feedback.
- Beware of seller's whose previous auction layout/terms differ from the current auction.
- Beware of any seller with unusual payment terms.
- Beware of any seller who has detailed procedures for payment that they insist must be followed.
- Beware of any seller who recommends an escrow company other than escrow.com
- Beware of any seller using bad grammar, posting in ALL CAPs, or who has obvious spelling errors in their auction.
- Beware of any seller who plays on the buyers emotions.
- Beware of any seller who insists on contact outside of eBay.
- Beware of any seller who suddenly changes their email address.
- Beware of any seller who claims their (email/PayPal/anything) is not working.
- NEVER send a Western Union payment for any auction!
- NEVER CLICK ON AN EMAIL LINK FOR PAYPAL OR EBAY!

Scam Check for Sellers

- Beware of any buyer who insists you ship before their payment clears.
- Beware of any buyer who sends more money than the amount due.
- Beware of any buyer who wants the item shipped to 'a friend'.
- Beware of any buyer who asks you personal questions.
- Beware of any buyer who suddenly changes their email address.
- Beware of any buyer who insists on paying by any unusual means or through an escrow company other than escrow.com.
- NEVER CLICK ON AN EMAIL LINK FOR PAYPAL OR EBAY!

Important Links

The latest Auction Safety Information and to report auction fraud visit
http://www.AuctionSafety.Org

Free toolbar to protect your eBay and PayPal accounts from spoof emails
http://www.MyLittleMole.com

Find out how to become an expert seller at
http://www.DontBidOnIt.com

CONTENTS

You were smart to pick up this book. It may save you thousands of dollars and it will surely make you a more educated eBay member. If it only saves you from being scammed once, it is well worth avoiding the headache and frustration.

EBay is a great place to buy and sell. I have used eBay since 1998 and I check my favorite categories everyday. I will continue to use it because I know what to look for and how to tread safely through the sometimes dangerous waters of Internet commerce.

Ebay and PayPal are highly secure sites. The problems occur with the people who use them. No one will ever obtain your eBay or PayPal passwords from those sites. They will obtain them from YOU! I will explain how scammers obtain your password without you knowing it and how you can protect yourself using free software.

Many of the same scams used on eBay are used on other websites, through the mail, and even in newspaper classifieds. Once you see how these scams work on eBay, you can apply the same knowledge to any website, any buyer, any seller. You may see some repetition because many scams are re-inventions of other scams or twists on old ideas. All scams have common threads. *If it sounds too good to be true*, applies to almost all of them.

We will start by discussing some basics about eBay and PayPal and what to do if your account is compromised. Everyone who is scammed asks '*How to I get my money/goods back?*", so we will answer that question too. Then we will look at specific scams and things to watch out for.

If you are ready to learn what scammers do not want you to know....turn the page.

If it sounds too good to be true...it is.

CHAPTER 1

VIOLATIONS

You can take every precaution and you can do everything right, but eventually you will have some kind of problem with a seller or buyer.

EBay is a big business with over a billion listings per year. They know that there will always be some bad sellers or bad buyers. There is no escaping that fact. They have setup a Security Center to handle these problems.

The Security Center lists policies, has links for customer support and links to file complaints. Purchases through eBay are automatically covered up to $200 per transaction minus a $25 deductible. There are some restrictions. You can find the latest terms on the eBay website. PayPal can offer protection up to $2000 on purchases made through their service. The coverage amount PayPal offers is listed in the auction under Payment Details.

Blow The Whistle!

It is important to report abuses and policy violations to eBay. EBay is a huge site and most of the listings are by-the-book honest listings. This can make it difficult for eBay to find the bad apples. They depend on the user community to let them know when an auction violates policy. It is very important for users to report non paying bidders and non receipt of goods as well as post appropriate feedback. This saves other members from the same bad experience. If you have a bad experience, it might have been avoided if previous members had followed through with feedback or complaints against the problem member. Good community members are on the watch for abuses of eBay.

Make sure what you are reporting is a violation of eBay policy. Just because someone left you negative feedback does not mean they violated any eBay policies.

What should be reported:

- Non Payment for an Auction – use the online form
- Non Receipt of Goods – contact seller first and if it is not resolved use the online form
- Significantly Not As Described – buyer receives an empty box or a used non-working item that was described as new.
- Spoof Messages – someone claims to be the seller and tries to trick you into redirecting payment to them
- Dealing Outside of EBay – A member offers to buy or sell outside of the protection of eBay
- Circumvention of eBay Fees – A seller offers a low listing price and extremely high shipping with a Buy-It-Now listing, a seller tries to make potential bidders contact them before bidding, a seller files a false non-payment notice.
- Unusual Bid Withdrawal – If you see a bidder suddenly retract a high bid just before the end of the auction, something is fishy.
- Inappropriate Contact – If another eBay user contacts you trying to sell you an item you are bidding on or another item, that is a violation of eBay rules. It is also spam and no one who sends spam can be trusted.
- Warning Off – When another eBay member sends a message to bidders of an auction claiming the seller is a crook or there is some other problem should not be trusted. These people may want to win the auction for themselves at a lower price or may simply be attacking the seller after a bad experience or negative feedback.
- Feedback Threats – a user threatens negative feedback if you do not leave them feedback or do not issue a refund or for any other undeserved reason.
- Invalid Email Address – If a user has a contact address that is bouncing email or they will not respond, this may indicate the user has bad contact information. Users are required to keep accurate and truthful contact information with eBay.
- Spam – If anyone sends you a message through the eBay Message Center that is not related to a transaction where they are trying to sell you something, trying to get you to go to a website, or trying to obtain personal information, should be reported to eBay immediately.
- Threats – if another user makes any physical threats they should be reported.
- Obscene Messages – If another member sends obscene, racist, vulgar or harassing messages, they should be reported to eBay.
- Listing Violations – an advertising or want-ad listed in the main eBay area, listing with no actual product offered for sale, items intentionally listed in the wrong categories, items using non-relevant keywords, brand name keywords of items not being sold in the auction.

When you need to report a violation, simply use the Report This Item link at the bottom of any auction page. You can use the Help Center search feature to find out if an activity is a violation of eBay rules without having to read the entire eBay rule book.

If you file a complaint that asks for comments or explanation, keep it short and stick to the facts. It is not necessary to give a long history. State the policy violation so the eBay monitor knows what to look for. That is all the Security Center needs to know. They are quite busy and do not have the time to read three paragraphs before finding the problem being reported. If you have any documentation, such as canceled checks, money order receipts, or emails, either include the information or let it be known these are available.

EBay does not usually notify you of the result. I have had them respond to let me know a user was suspended on some offences. Most of the time there is no notice. EBay may send the offender a nasty email or suspend their account. If the violation is serious they may turn the matter over to law enforcement. Civil matters will not be turned over to law enforcement, but if you decide to sue another member, the complaint may be used in court if you should decide to sue a dishonest member. This is another good reason to keep your comments and descriptions limited to the facts. If it becomes evidence later, you do not want to be embarrassed reading your comments in court.

Filing a complaint may or may not resolve the problem. It depends on the nature of the problem and the evidence eBay has. EBay can't do much if another member emails a threat outside of eBay, but they can if a threat is sent using the eBay message center. EBay has no control or authority over your personal email; only over their message center. Though imperfect, it is the system we have to use.

If you have a problem with a member who does have their account suspended, I suggest you change your user ID. This can make it harder for them to find you if they should re-register later using new information.

If you do have a problem with a user who is suspended, and then suddenly have new problems with a new zero feedback member who has the New icon by their ID, you can bet this is the same person. You can report them to eBay again and eBay can verify their information and the IP address they are using to connect to eBay. Add the new problem bidder to your blocked bidder list too.

CHAPTER 2

BUSINESS VS SCAMMERS

Why do eBay and PayPal not stop the scams?

EBay and PayPal want to limit fraud as much as possible. They both have extensive security departments that are constantly reviewing suspect activity. They also want to make the sign up process and bidding process as easy as possible. If the sign up process is too hard, many people will abandon it and never become members. Imagine going to your local grocery store and having to walk through a metal detector, then show ID and sit in a waiting room while it was verified, then answer several security questions about your bank account, your credit card, and your address. You may be in a very secure grocery store, but would you go back? Most people would not. Too much security drives away customers.

If a bidder is ripped off in one of their first three transactions on eBay, they will likely never return. EBay wants members to return. This is why eBay works to keep their site a safe and fair marketplace. They do not want to lose members. At the same time they do not want to prevent members from joining.

If you have been using the Internet very long then you have no doubt seen complaints about eBay and PayPal. The majority of these complaints fall into two categories. They are either baseless because the person making the accusation failed to follow or understand the rules, or the person making the accusation could have avoided the problem by following the advice in this program.

I think it is very important to clarify some of these complaints so you are not misled into thinking criminals are running rampant. They are not. EBay and PayPal are extremely safe places to do business, but, as with any transaction on or off the Internet, you must exercise common sense and be cautious.

Let's look at the extremes of buyer and seller protection. If PayPal or eBay guaranteed no payment reversals by buyers, sellers would love it. Honest sellers would never have to worry about dishonest buyers reversing payments. But, scam sellers could freely sell anything. They never would have to deliver, just collect money. This protection measure becomes a license to steal.

If instant no questions asked payment reversals were available, buyers would love it. Honest buyers would never have to worry about dishonest sellers because they can always reverse the payment. Then every small time criminal and dishonest person could buy any item they wanted and file for a reversal on the payment. They can buy thousands of dollars in goods and never actually pay for anything. This protection measure has now become a license to steal.

When you give total protection to one side of the transaction, it can be abused. There is no way to give total protection to both sides. PayPal and eBay must choose something in between these extremes. No matter what system is chosen, someone will always be dissatisfied.

PayPal and eBay must consider their own businesses when making policies. If either company changed to a 100% no fraud guarantee, they would both be out of business in a week. The scammers would change their tactics and begin filing millions of fake claims.

This is how a bad transaction usually happens. A buyer sends payment to a seller. Two weeks later the charge is reversed by the buyer claiming non-receipt. The seller failed to ship by a trackable means so they cannot provide proof of delivery. The payment is returned to the buyer. The seller goes to every website they can to complain how PayPal unfairly took money out of their account and how PayPal ripped them off. The seller does not want to accept any responsibility for their failure to provide proof of shipment. Shipping goods by a trackable means is one of the requirements in the PayPal policy. PayPal did not file the reversal, the buyer did. Yet, the seller thinks PayPal should absorb the cost for every fraudulent transaction. That is hardly fair and it would not be in the interest of PayPal or PayPal's customers. The seller also failed to follow the PayPal procedure which would have protected him.

I do not want you to be fooled by such misleading or one sided complaints. It is important that you understand in more detail exactly how PayPal works and what you should expect from them.

PayPal handles the money just like a bank. It says this in the first paragraph of their policy. They are not responsible for the quality of the items sold. They are not responsible for the goods and never vouched for the honesty of the buyer or seller. They are an intermediary. Claiming PayPal should reimburse anyone who is defrauded is the equivalent of saying your local bank should repay anyone who is the victim of a crime. Many people simply do not understand, or do not think about, what PayPal's is responsible for. PayPal is a payment service. It is not an escrow service and they are not selling anything. This misunderstanding leads to many unfounded complaints. Many people blame PayPal for not offering services they never claimed to offer.

Some people try to hold PayPal accountable for matters that have nothing to do with PayPal. If a transaction goes bad, it is not automatically PayPal's, or eBay's responsibility to cover the cost.

A buyer may send a payment to a seller through PayPal using their credit card. Then if the seller does not ship or if the buyer is simply dissatisfied, they may violate the PayPal rules they agreed to when sending the payment and file a chargeback on their credit card and accuse PayPal of fraud for not recovering their money from a dishonest seller. The buyer who filed the chargeback is actually the one committing fraud.

I like examples so here is a comparison that I think will make the chargeback situation clear.

When someone provides a checking account number or credit card number to PayPal, they are authorizing PayPal to charge their credit card or bank account and add money to their PayPal account. It is just like writing a check for deposit to your savings account. Money is transferred from one place to another. The person is not paying for a purchase with their credit card. They are transferring money with it. Once the money is in their PayPal account, it can be applied to a purchase. This is no different from depositing a pay-check at the bank. On Friday a person gives their pay-check to their bank to add credit to their bank account. Then they mail a check from their account to the seller. When the seller receives the check, he deposits it in his bank and the money is taken from the buyer's account. The bank is not responsible for who the buyer writes a check to and the bank has no obligation to recover the money if the buyer receives nothing for their purchase or is dissatisfied with the item they receive.

At the bank, the person is authorizing the bank to deposit the check to their account. At PayPal, the person is authorizing a transfer to their PayPal account from their credit card. Reversing the charge later is fraud. Paypal met their obligations by adding the credit to the person's PayPal account. The bank met its obligation by depositing the pay-check to the person's account. Paypal is not responsible for the person sending money to a scammer any more than a bank is responsible for a person writing a check to a scammer. Many people will try to hold PayPal accountable for their own decisions when they would never consider going to their bank and demanding money back for a check they mailed to a scammer.

If that example was not clear, then lets look at this one.

A buyer wins an auction and purchases a money order at the post office using their credit card. The postal clerk issues a money order for $100. The buyer now has exactly what they requested, a $100 money order. Their business with the post office is finished. The buyer sends the money order to the seller. The buyer never receives anything from the seller. Now the buyer files a complaint with their credit card company to reverse the $100 charge made by the post office. Did the post office defraud the buyer? No, the post office fulfilled their obligation and turned over a good money order to the buyer. The buyer was not scammed by the post office. The buyer has committed fraud by filing a false chargeback request with their credit card company. The buyer received what they purchased, a money order. What the buyer did with it after they left the post office is not the post office's responsibility. This is why the post office does not actually accept credit card payments for money orders. Once a buyer makes a deposit to PayPal, whether by bank account or credit card, it is then the buyer who requests PayPal send money to a seller. It is not PayPal's responsibility to determine if the seller is legitimate before sending the payment. They are acting on the instructions of the buyer. Instead of using a post office, the buyer in our example used PayPal and requested they electronically transfer funds instead of using a money order. PayPal is no more responsible for who the buyer chooses to send a payment to than the post office is responsible for who the buyer mails a money order to.

I think another example is in order because there is so much confusion about this issue on the Internet.

A buyer purchases an auction item and selects PayPal as the payment method. The buyer uses their credit card to fund the purchase. They are not paying the seller with their credit card. The buyer is authorizing PayPal to take money from their credit card and place this money in their PayPal account. This is no different from depositing money in the bank or buying a money order. PayPal does exactly as requested and credits the buyer's PayPal account. The buyer then requests the money in their account be transferred to the seller. The buyer receives their purchase, but they are dissatisfied with the color. The purchase does not qualify for PayPal protection because PayPal does not guarantee the quality of the goods. PayPal cannot guarantee the quality of the goods because they are only handling the money and have nothing to do with the goods. PayPal denies the buyer's claim because the goods were delivered according to PayPal's policy. Now the buyer files a chargeback on their credit card. Was the buyer defrauded by PayPal? No, PayPal has nothing to do with the buyer's dissatisfaction with the item. PayPal did exactly as the buyer instructed. They transferred money to the buyer's account from the credit card provided by the buyer and PayPal transferred money from the buyer's PayPal account to the seller as the buyer requested. When the buyer files a credit card chargeback, they have committed fraud because PayPal did nothing wrong.

PayPal rules clearly state that payments funded by credit card cannot be reversed. The buyer agreed to these terms when they made the payment. The buyer broke the agreement by filing a reversal. The buyer could have filed a complaint through PayPal if the item was not received or significantly not as described and attempt to legitimately recover their money. The buyer could also have returned the goods.

If a buyer wants the 100% fraud protection of their credit card, they will need to pay the seller directly by credit card. Buyers should never file a chargeback against PayPal. Not only is this against the terms the buyer agreed to when sending the payment, it is fraud on the part of the buyer.

Now that you understand why it is wrong to file a chargeback for payments funded through PayPal with a credit card, you will have a better understanding of the blog complaints and rants you find on the Internet and a better understanding of how PayPal works.

PayPal has no way to determine if scammers are filing false claims now and attempting to take over both sides of the transaction. When a customer calls to complain that their account was shut down because they received a fraudulent credit card payment, they never think about how the transaction looks to PayPal. Is the person complaining actually the scammer trying to open the account so they can transfer out the stolen money? Is this person's son the actual scammer?

Suppose you sell an item to a buyer on eBay who pays by PayPal. Then PayPal finds out this buyer has committed fraud and accessed other people's PayPal accounts. His PayPal account will be disabled, along with all of the accounts that he or his associates may have access to. This includes any accounts that he has received money from or sent money to. PayPal cannot see who sent the payments, only what accounts were used. This means your account could be disabled because you sold to the wrong person. This is not a common occurrence, but it is a possibility. PayPal cannot allow an account to continue operating if there is a possibility the scammer may be the one controlling it. Freezing suspect accounts is necessary to protect both PayPal and honest PayPal members. The accounts are unfrozen when the members identities are confirmed.

Suppose PayPal receives a complaint from a buyer saying the seller never shipped anything. How can they prove something did not happen? They cannot. Someone must prove 'something' did happen. This is why the seller must prove shipment and delivery with a tracking number. PayPal notifies the seller and freezes the money transferred in the transaction. If the seller is unable to prove they shipped the item or ignores the notice, then who is at fault? It is easy for the seller to *say* they shipped, but they need to show proof.

A receipt is not proof. Anyone can print out a receipt or Photoshop a perfect copy; one that is even nicer than a real receipt. A digital image or even an original receipt proves nothing even if you have a forensics team available to analyze it. PayPal has no choice but to return the money to the buyer if the seller cannot prove they shipped according to the PayPal rules. To the seller it will appear unfair. The seller may begin posting rants in their auctions about how they were ripped off by PayPal, but they take no responsibility for their own failure to follow the rules PayPal set out to protect buyers and sellers. The buyer, who never received the item, believes PayPal saved them from fraud so the buyer is very happy with PayPal. The buyer however, will not go around to message boards proclaiming how they were protected by PayPal. They will go about their lives and may not mention the incident to anyone.

Sometimes talking on the phone to an service representative is not enough. If a scammer has obtained your personal information, they can just as easily answer questions about your address, name, and credit cards as you can. If PayPal or eBay reactivated every account simply because someone called saying they were the real account owner, the amount of fraud would double. Scammers would realize they could call, act angry, and give some basic information to have their victim's account re-enabled so they can commit more scams.

"I called and said Mr. X. was running a scam and should be shut down, but they were not helpful".

EBay or PayPal would be foolish to disable the account. This call could be from an ex-boyfriend or girlfriend trying to shutdown the legitimate owners account. It could be a dishonest business trying to shutdown the account of their competition. Simply asking for someone's account to be shut down or making an accusation is not enough. This can make it appear that eBay or PayPal are protecting scammers, but without proof of wrongdoing or a specific rule violation, they cannot take any action.

One of the biggest reasons for complaints on the Internet about PayPal or eBay is a poor understanding of how their policies work. People tend to see the world from their personal perspective; how does this affect me. They do not consider why the policies are the way they are.

Here are some common examples of Internet complaints.

I received an e-mail from paypal saying that they had suspended my account because I had registered by using another person's identity. They then said that I had 72 hours to confirm my identity or my account would be cancelled. They then provided a link to the form I needed to fill out, but when I clicked on it, I found out that the link didn't exist. Why would they accuse me of not being me, then not giving me an actual way to prove myself?

What has happened in this email will be very clear when you finish this book. This person is blaming PayPal when PayPal had absolutely nothing to do with the problem. This person received a fake email that only looked like it was from PayPal. Fortunately for this person, the website was caught and disabled before she gave away her password. There was never a problem with her account, it was all part of a scam and had nothing to do with PayPal.

I had a buyer pay me $2000 dollars through paypal and ask that I overnight the music keyboard. I did and the next day the payment was reversed. Supposedly the account was stolen. How is that my fault. Paypal's system was compromised and I lose $2k. BEWARE Ebay or Paypal has no protection for sellers.

Actually eBay and PayPal offer lots of protection, but this seller chose not to follow their protection rules. The seller did not ship to the Confirmed address. If the seller had insisted on a Confirmed address, the scam buyer would not be able to provide one without the item going to the real account owner. They also assume PayPal's system was compromised, but the account owner is most likely the one to blame. This situation is the equivalent of someone robbing a bank, then crossing the street and buying a get-away car, and the car dealership complaining about having to give the money back. To the seller, it can easily appear that PayPal allows fraud, but to the original account owner, it appears PayPal protected them from fraud. If PayPal had not reversed the transaction, the account owner might be the one posting a complaint. There are always two sides to these situations.

I am another victim of paypal. They froze my whole account, because an ebay buyer hadn't received their item yet. The customer would have gotten their item, but it was on backorder and I had directly contacted the customer and spoke with him...

This is an example of an inexperienced seller. They sold an item they did not have and began making excuses to the buyer. As you will see later, the buyer did exactly what they should have done, filed a complaint. Also, this person appears to be stretching the truth. If a single customer filed a single chargeback, the seller's account would not be frozen. Only the involved funds would be on hold. There is more to this story than the seller is admitting. The buyer believes, with good reason, they are about to be the victims of fraud. The buyer paid for something, the seller has not shipped anything and is delaying the buyer with excuses. The buyer believes they just avoided being ripped off thanks to PayPal. PayPal is trying to protect other buyers by disabling this seller's account.

My ebay account was cancelled for no reason. I had been selling a CD. Lots of other people are offering the same CD right now but my account was cancelled not theirs. Maybe it was a set of ebooks but so what.

These types of posts are always entertaining. The poster first says their account was disabled for no reason, then they reveal they were selling illegal pirate copies of books or software on CD which is not only against eBay rules, it is against the law. They try to justify their violation of the law by claiming other people are doing it. EBay's policy protects the owners of intellectual property and requires members obey the law.

CHAPTER 3

If your password is compromised (someone finds out what it is), the scammer can hijack your account. They can login and post fraudulent auctions on eBay or make unauthorized money transfers using PayPal if they have your PayPal password.

Bad guys can post fake auctions using your account in an attempt to use your good feedback to scam buyers. If the bad guy knows you and wants to attack you personally, they can post false feedback for other members, post auctions that violate eBay policy, or bid on expensive items using your account. They may post fake auctions for expensive items to run up your eBay fees. Avoid all of these problems by keeping your passwords secret.

Friends and family can and do abuse accounts. Make sure current boyfriend/girlfriend does not know your password. When they become ex's you can avoid a problem and you will be glad you kept your password secure. You should never share your password with anyone including family and friends. No one has any legitimate reason to even ask for your eBay or PayPal password. You may be very careful with your password, but your friends may not be so careful and enter them in look-alike websites. Your password is for you and you alone.

If you think your password has been compromised, or just suspect someone may know what it is, immediately change it. Don't wait. Don't hope for the best. Login to your account and change it right then. It it will cause you lots of problems if you do not quickly change your password to prevent others from accessing your account.

What do you do if your eBay or PayPal account has been hijacked?

The first thing to do is act fast. You cannot wait for a response from eBay or PayPal. You have to do something now. If you cannot login to your account, you can reset your password using the '*Forgot Password*' link on eBay or PayPal. This link will ask you to verify your security question and will email a new password to the primary account email address.

If either your eBay or PayPal account is compromised, assume the other may also have been compromised.

If you think your account has been compromised:

* Change your email address for eBay and PayPal if the scammer changed them to something other than *your* email addresses. Make a note of what the scammer's addresses are.
* Change your passwords for eBay and PayPal. If one is compromised, the other may also be compromised. Use the *Forgot Password* link to reset the password if you cannot log in.
* Check your bank information, address and phone numbers.
* Change your security question.

- Check any auctions you have listed and make sure only your auctions are listed and that the content of those auctions has not changed.
- Check your PayPal account balance and look for unfamiliar transactions.
- Now, contact eBay through the Live Help link on their main page or PayPal's security center through their website. PayPal's security center phone number is in the appendix. If you are an eBay Power Seller, you will have a special support number you can call too. Make sure you let them know you changed the password and any other information that was changed.

EBay and PayPal request that you select a security question. If you forget your password, they can use the answer to this question to verify that you are who you claim to be. They can then reset your password to a new temporary password.

You may be too late and find the bad guy has changed your password to something new as well as your security question, locking you out of your account. If this happens, go to the Live Help section of eBay from their main page and explain what has happened. If your PayPal password has been compromised, call their support number or email directly or both. You can minimize the damage and maybe lock the accounts to prevent the bad guy from using them until everything is straightened out.

Check for any bank transfers to or from the bank account linked in your PayPal account. Check your personal information to see if the scammer changed the name, address, phone, bank account, or other details. Check your Closed Auction list under MyEBay to see if the scammer has already completed any auctions using your account. Tell any buyers of fraudulent auctions not to send payment.

Keep a written log of everything that has happened, the time, date, auction numbers, and what you did to stop or correct it. Print out screenshots of the scammers activity using File/Print from your browser. Documentation may be important later for eBay or PayPal investigations or for law enforcement. Write down any changes before changing them back. Make sure you change the password FIRST; otherwise the scammer may log into your account and see the changes you have made.

EBay or PayPal may offer the option to freeze your account. This should not be necessary if you were able to login to your account and change the password or you recovered the password using the security question. If you have access to your account and you have changed the password, there is no reason to freeze it.

Scammers frequently do not change eBay or PayPal email addresses. The real account owner receives a notification email when the primary email is changed. This alerts the real owner someone has accessed their account. Scammers do not want to tip off the legitimate owners so they usually do not change contact email addresses.

Most of the time, an account compromise results from the account owner clicking a link in an email that goes to a look-alike website. The website may look exactly like PayPal or eBay, but it is not. The website is a fake setup by the scammer. The password goes straight to the scammer as soon as it is entered. The visitor is then either asked for additional information, forwarded to the real site, or told the system is down for maintenance. These links may come in email messages or they may be in real auctions.

When you receive an email from eBay or PayPal, never click a link in the email. NEVER!

For that matter, you should never click any link in any email because almost all links in email are to fraudulent websites.

If you are careful with your passwords, you are careful to only enter them into the real eBay or PayPal websites, and you do not share them with family or friends, you should have no security problems with your account.

You can use the Live Help link on the eBay main webpage at eBay.com to contact support. EBay uses the live help chat feature instead of phone support because it is much more efficient. Live Help online support saves eBay time and allows their operator to help several people at once.

NON CRIMINAL PROBLEMS

Not every problem on eBay is related to outright criminal fraud. There are problems with non-paying bidders and sellers who may not be completely honest in their dealings or a forgetful member.

EBay will not make another member complete a transaction. They can only send a warning or suspend the member if you offer an item for sale and the buyer refuses to pay. EBay will not force the member to honor their legal agreement. You do have the option of taking the member to court to enforce the bid contract, but when you are selling $20 and $50 items, court is not an economical alternative. Small Claims court can be useful for smaller claims and you can ask for punitive damages above the cost of the actual item.

MEDIATION

You can elect to resolve a problem through Square Trade's mediators. There are two steps, the first involves the buyer and seller self mediating. This is no different than emailing each other. The members enter their message in a mediation console page and that sends the message to the other person. It is a way of contacting the other member without feeling like you are contacting them directly. The next stage goes to mediation before a live person. You have to pay for this privilege. Square Trade is an eBay recommended and owned service that mediates disputes between buyers and sellers.

This requires both parties be reasonable and willing to go through mediation. In my experience, if the parties are reasonable they can work out the issue on their own. Most of the time one or the other party is unwilling to resolve the matter or stops responding to mediation when they become tired of the process.

You are generally better off trying to resolve the matter yourself. If that is not successful, it is possible the other party may feel more pressure if Square Trade sends them 'official' emails once you start the mediation process.

Mediation is of no use if you have been scammed by a professional criminal or if you purchased from a hijacked account. The account owner was not the seller so they have no reason to use mediation.

INSURANCE

EBay and PayPal do not offer insurance. They do offer member protection for items that were not received or that were misrepresented. Coverage, for both eBay and PayPal, can depend on the payment method, item, and the country involved. Protection does not cover items that may have been lost or damaged in shipping. EBay coverage covers up to $175($200 minus $25 deductible). The deductible helps eBay avoid dealing with thousands of small claims. You can find details about eBay's coverage in the eBay Help Center.

PayPal's policy is a bit complicated. You can find details on their website. They offer a tiered coverage system that can range from $200 to $2000 or more or it may cover nothing. The easy way to determine what PayPal covers is to look at the auction. Auctions will show their coverage for PayPal payments.

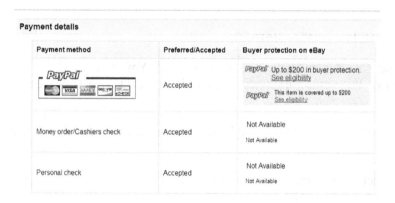

Auctions paid using PayPal show the amount of coverage in the auction listing.

CHAPTER 5

I'VE BEEN SCAMMED

It is always best to contact the other party to resolve the matter first. If you have not used the Message Center to contact the other party, do that before filing a complaint. Most of the time you will find there was a misunderstanding or possibly a slow shipping seller to blame and not fraudulent intent. Filing a PayPal or eBay complaint against a seller who has done nothing wrong can make resolving the matter much more difficult. The package may have been lost in the mail and filing a complaint without contacting the seller first may make the seller less cooperative.

HOW DO I GET MY MONEY BACK?

You won and paid for an item that never arrived. You contacted the seller and they do not respond or they make excuses. It has been ten days to two weeks since you sent payment.

It's official. You have been scammed and there is no question about it. What do you do now?

How do you get your money back!!!! You may not. Then again, if you paid using PayPal or a credit card there is hope.

> *If you have fallen victim to a scam and the criminal obtained your personal information such as credit cards, bank account numbers, or other financial information, there are nonprofit organizations that offer advice and assistance. Two of the largest are*
>
> *The Privacy Rights Clearinghouse http://www.privacyrights.org/ and the Identity Theft Resource Center http://www.idtheftcenter.org.*

What if your purchase never arrives?

Sellers can make mistakes. I have sent payment and the seller did not realize it was in their PayPal account. Sometimes it happens. A seller has ten auctions to ship and the wrong label goes on the right box.

If your item does not arrive in a reasonable time, you should contact the seller. Priority Mail packages in the US should arrive about one week after you have sent payment. This gives the seller a couple of days to ship the item and at least three days for delivery. I usually wait ten days before I start to worry. Some sellers can be slow to ship or may only ship on certain days of the week. Always be polite when you contact the seller. There may have been some crossed wires that delayed your order. Ask the status of the shipment and if the seller has a tracking number using the eBay Message Console. The seller should reply within 2 or 3 days. If they do not respond, this is a bad sign. Take another look at the seller's feedback. Has it changed? Are there suddenly a lot of negative ratings? Do you still trust the seller? If I paid for a package and ten days have passed, then the seller does not reply to a Message Center request for shipping status, I immediately file for a PayPal refund at the PayPal.com website. Honest sellers will respond to eBay Message Center questions.

If it is clearly fraud, you can file a PayPal non-receipt claim and recover all of the money if the seller does not prove the item was shipped and delivered. PayPal complaints must be filed within 30 days after the payment is sent. PayPal offers up to $2000 in protection with some restrictions. You can find details on PayPal's protection at PayPal.com

There are two options when filing a PayPal complaint. The default option simply emails between the buyer and seller as each respond on the PayPal site. This keeps an official record of communications and any efforts to resolve the matter by either party. PayPal only becomes involved when the complaint is Escalated. If a complaint is not escalated, it will eventually expire and nothing will be done. When a complaint is first filed, the money is not frozen. If you have been scammed, then you should escalate the complaint immediately to prevent the scammer from taking the money out of their PayPal account.

If the seller does not respond to the PayPal complaint, you should receive your payment back. If the seller has cleaned out their PayPal account, you may not receive your money back. PayPal does not guarantee your money back. They only promise a 'best effort'.

Also file an eBay complaint for 'Item Not Received' in the Security Center section of eBay or if the item was misrepresented file a 'Seller Non-Performance' complaint. It is important to file a report so eBay can take appropriate action and save other buyers from the same problems you experienced.

A 'Seller Non-Performance' complaint is similar to the Non-Paying Bidder notice, but it is against sellers who misrepresent the goods or back out of the auction. The buyer cannot file a complaint if the buyer does not honor the terms of auction. If the auction states that the seller accepts PayPal only and the buyer wants to send a money order, the seller does not have to complete the transaction because the buyer bid based on the listed terms and then tried to alter those terms. Sellers are not required to sell if the auction is a reserve auction and the high bid does not meet the reserve. Otherwise if a seller backs out because the final auction price was too low, the seller misrepresented the item, or they simply do not ship, you should file a Seller Non-Performance notice.

You can only file a complaint once per transaction at PayPal. If you file a non-receipt complaint and the seller assures you it is on the way and you cancel the complaint, you cannot re-file it later if the item does not show up. Leave the complaint pending until you receive what you paid for.

There is no point in sending message after message trying to reach an unresponsive seller. If the seller does not respond to the second message asking the status, they are not going to respond to a a third and if they do not respond to the third, they will definitely not respond to any other requests. Don't waste time sending 'please respond' type messages. A legitimate seller responds to questions within 1 or 2 business days(not necessarily weekends). Sometimes emails are overlooked and the seller may not see your message in the Message Center so it is a good idea to send a second message.

I have been on eBay since 1998 and out of thousands of transactions, I have only filed a PayPal refund request a few times. Every PayPal refund request was successfully resolved except one in which I lost $120. This was one of the first purchases I made on eBay. I should have filed a claim with eBay and I could have recovered the money there, but I did not know I could do file at the time.

If you paid with a check, call your bank and request a 'stop payment'. If the check has been cashed, it is too late. If you think you sent a check to a professional criminal, you should either freeze that account for six months or close it and open a new account. Scammers can take the information from your check and print more checks on your account. They may even use the numbers to make payments to websites that accept eChecks which means they do not have to bother printing checks.

If you paid with a money order, call the customer service number on the receipt and request a '**stop payment**' for a stolen money order. A Stop Payment prevents the scammer from cashing it. If they are a scammer then it is stolen because it was obtained under false pretense. If the money order has been cashed already, there is nothing that the money order company can do. You can still file a mail fraud complaint with the Postal Inspectors.

If you paid by credit card and did not use a Virtual Number, cancel the card and reverse the charge. If you followed the <u>Don't Bid On It</u> program advice, you used a virtual card number so the scammer cannot use the number again and it will not be necessary to cancel the card. You can usually obtain a one time use virtual credit card number, through the website for your credit card company. You should always use virtual card numbers for eBay purchases which are paid by credit card directly to the seller.

If the scammer has your Social Security Number, contact the major credit bureaus and have a credit watch or lock placed on your accounts. This may sound extreme, but you do not know who scammed you. Was it a small time crook after $50 or was it someone connected or organized crime who will try to sell your information for identity theft and more credit card fraud. Small time crooks rarely ask for your Social Security Number. You can request a lock to prevent new credit being issued. This is not necessary unless the scammer has your Social Security Number. There are services that will monitor your credit records for abuse. You should never give anyone your Social Security Number.

If you sent payment by Western Union, the money is gone, unless the scammer has not yet picked up the money. You can contact Western Union and have the payment stopped and reversed so you can recover it. You should never pay for an auction using Western Union.

If you sent payment by bank transfer, contact your bank and attempt to reverse the payment. Then call the destination bank yourself, or sit there while your bank calls them, and notify them that one of their accounts is being used for fraud. They may be able to freeze the account and return your money. This only works if you can freeze the account before the scammer cleans it out.

Cash payments offer no proof of payment and it will not be recoverable. It may be tempting to drop a $20 bill in an envelope to pay for an inexpensive auction, but it is not a wise thing to do and it is against postal regulations to ship currency in regular mail.

Beware of spam soon after being scammed which offers to 'help' you recover your money or your goods. These are sent by the same scammer who originally scammed the victim. They will attempt to obtain service fees or to obtain additional personal information they can use to steal the victims identity.

Your credit card company, PayPal and EBay are your most likely avenues for recovering lost money. This is especially true if the amount involved is small and you act fast. The good news is that fraud is not common considering the number of transactions each company handles every day.

There is always a risk when buying from someone else, whether it is on eBay, through a newspaper classified ad, a magazine ad, or a swap meet. Most of the time transactions go without a hitch.

If you decide to go beyond eBay and PayPal, such as to the police or a lawyer, make sure the person you are filing a complaint against is the actual crook. If a scammer hijacked an eBay or PayPal account, the account owner is also a victim. Just because the eBay personal information for your seller says the account belongs to John Smith, it does not mean John Smith was the person posting the auctions. It could have been an account hijacker.

You can find a list of contacts in the Appendix for sites where you can file complaints and find more information on mail fraud. You can also find the latest updated shortcuts at
http://portal.dont-bid-on-it.com

EBay Forums and Chat Rooms

One of the best resources, at least emotionally if not legally, are the eBay forums. Here members can meet and chat about many topics associated with eBay. You can find more current information on fraud and how to deal with it. You may find others who are having problems with the same buyer or seller. You can search the forums to see if your question has been asked before. Most of the time, it has already been asked by many other members and answered many times. You can find the forums by clicking on the Community link at the top of any eBay page.

How do I get my goods back?

You sold something and the check bounced or PayPal reversed the payment due to a stolen credit card being used. How do you get your stuff back?

There is less protection for sellers who are defrauded by buyers. If you have a business and receive many checks, you can use a check service that will automatically collect on bad checks when money is placed in the person's checking account. That is assuming the buyer ever puts money in their account.

Professional criminals will be the most difficult to track down. The mildly dishonest member will be easier to track down.

Sellers can file an eBay Non-Payment complaint and hope to have the buyer's account disabled.

If a seller shipped to the PayPal Verified address of the buyer, they may have some protection. PayPal will even attempt to recover the funds if the buyer paid by credit card and reversed the charges as long as the card number was not stolen.

Beyond eBay and PayPal, your best options are small claims court or turn the matter over to a collections agency. It is unlikely you will ever recover the goods, but you may be able to force the buyer to pay for what they purchased.

Occasionally the local police may be helpful. Before filing a lawsuit or contacting the police, make sure you know who scammed you. The account used to bid on your item may have been hijacked. As I said, the person who owns the account may not be the person you were dealing with.

If the item has not been delivered, you may be able to redirect the package or recall the package if you shipped by UPS or FedEx.

Sometimes a loss is the cost of doing business. You want to make payments and transactions as easy as possible to generate the most sales, but in doing so you open the door to some dishonest buyers.

Federalies

The Big Guns

What if you have been defrauded and filing a PayPal or eBay complaint is not an option? If the payment was sent through the mail or the goods are shipped through the mail, you can report the seller to the US Postal Inspectors. Sending payment by mail and not receiving anything is mail fraud. Sending an item that is significantly not as described can also be mail fraud. You can find the latest information and procedures on filing a complaint at

> http://www.usps.com/postalinspectors/

You must file a postal inspector complaint within 90 days. Shipping records are only kept for 90 days. After that time, you will not be able to prove your payment was sent or received and the postal inspectors will no longer investigate.

The FBI will not investigate small claims. They will only look into cases that involve $100,000 or more. Even if the total amount of fraud against several buyers or sellers is over $100,000, it is unlikely they will investigate.

ATTORNEY GENERAL

You can file a complaint with the attorney general for the state the seller lives in. They will be more likely to respond if you are having problems with a business. Don't expect to send them a complaint and have everything taken care of. You will likely have to either provide a lot of information or do some investigating on your own. I have found that complaints are often closed with the response *'unable to contact the other party'*. That basically means they called or sent a letter and the crook didn't respond so they are giving up.

BETTER BUSINESS BUREAU

The BBB will not be helpful. They only collect information and offer advice on business related scams. Not auction scams. The BBB does have information on a number of sellers who have eBay Stores which may be helpful. Companies pay to be listed at the BBB. The BBB is not a government organization. The BBB does not enforce laws. Businesses pay to join the BBB and they can pay the BBB to have negative reviews "adjusted" so they do not affect the company rating.

LOCAL POLICE

If the seller is in the same city or same state, you may find help from your local police. If the seller is in another state, your local police may be unwilling or unable to help. They cannot investigate every $50 fraud case or they would have no time to do more serious work. Your local police will tell you to file a report with the police in the scammer's city. The police in the scammer's city will tell you to file a report with your local police. Many criminals depend on this.

If you were burglarized and see an item on eBay that was stolen from you and you have no doubt it is the exact item, immediately place a very high bid to prevent anyone from winning it or from using a Buy It Now price. You can request the seller's personal information, but that may tip them off. If you wait until the end of the auction and ask to pay cash on pickup, the crook may reveal their information willingly. Then show up with the police at the agreed meeting place. Maybe the crook will even give his home address. You should not go alone, always contact the police.

If you can find the real name of the person who scammed you, or if you hire a private investigator who can find the real name, you can provide this to a detective in this scammer's city. If the person has other complaints or is on parole/probation, this small case may suddenly be interesting to the local police. If you can show this person violated parole/probation, they may be sent back to jail.

FTC

The Federal Trade Commission will accept complaints, but generally only investigates large scale fraud activities or repeat criminals. Filing a report through their website goes into a statistics database, not an investigations file. Don't expect to recover your $100 for that gold plated radiator cap that never arrived from Brazil either. They will not investigate matters outside the USA.

The FTC receives thousands of complaints daily and many regarding PayPal and eBay. This is a matter of numbers because these companies generate so many transactions. The FTC is deluged with complaints and the majority of them are baseless. The claims involve members who failed to follow the refund rules, members who gave away or shared their passwords and then blame eBay or PayPal. These reports have nothing to do with PayPal or eBay. It becomes very difficult for the FTC to investigate legitimate cases with such reports piling up.

Lawyers

You have the option of filing a civil lawsuit if you are scammed by a seller who does not ship the goods or a buyer who refuses to pay.

You will need an attorney who is familiar with Internet law if you choose to file a lawsuit against the scammer. Many lawyers still do not know how to use email. Make sure you find one who understands how the Internet works. You can also learn a lot about the law by filing the suit yourself and only using a lawyer for advice. Before contacting a lawyer, make sure you know who the scammer is. If the eBay account was hijacked, the person you sent money to was not the person who owns the account. A lawyer will not be helpful if you were scammed by someone in Romania. It simply is not worth the cost to recover the money.

You can find qualified lawyers through local lawyers. They are usually glad to refer a friend or colleague and their referral may even know something about the law. You can also use online legal resources like LawFind.com. If your seller took the money and did not ship or the buyer did not pay, that is a simple Breach of Contract case in the civil law world. If the case is strong and the lawyer thinks they can collect, they may take the case on a contingency basis. You would not have to pay up front. They would only do this on a high priced item. The cost of the lawyer would be more than the value of the item if you purchased a $100 gold plated radiator cap.

You will have to file your lawsuit in the county in which you live. This is where the crime or breach occurred. If you win your case, then you will have to file additional papers in the county of the scammer asking their court system to honor the judgement of your local court system.

It will be important to have printouts of all of the webpages and your hand written record of the events. Always ask for punitive damages. Punitive damages are meant to punish the offender. If you are lucky, you may collect a few thousand dollars for that $500 auction item if you can show that the non paying bidder intentionally violated the bid contract.

Collecting that money...that is something I will leave for your lawyer to explain.

FAVORITE BAD SELLERS

You may not find satisfaction in simply filing an eBay complaint if you have been scammed.

Add the bad seller to your 'favorite sellers' list. I know they may not be your favorite, but every time they list an item for auction you will be notified by email. You can then check their auctions carefully for violations. Suppose you were scammed by a seller who had excessive shipping costs and a low Buy-It-Now price. The seller will likely continue to use this same method. You can report the seller when you see them commit the same offence and have their auctions cancelled. If the seller then relists the same auctions with the same excessive shipping rates, you will receive an email notice about the auctions and can report the new violations again. If you look carefully you may even see other violations. Dishonest sellers often violate more than one rule. Circumvention of eBay fees, such as excessive shipping, or offering to sell an item outside of eBay will gain a faster and more serious response than some other listing violations. These violations cost eBay money and eBay does not like that. They are less forgiving of these violations. If you have the choice between reporting someone for offering to sell an item outside of eBay and reporting them for spamming keywords, go with the outside-eBay report, it will get a faster response. You can report both offences.

APPEALING A DENIED PAYPAL CLAIM

Very few people know that you can appeal a denied PayPal claim. Generally, PayPal will not issue a refund for a misrepresented item and will automatically deny any such claim. Once a claim is denied, it cannot be re-filed.

This is how it usually goes: you receive the item and it is a new reproduction, not an original antique as claimed in the auction. The seller refuses to take a return or issue a refund. You file a PayPal complaint which is automatically denied because you selected 'not as described'. You ship the item back to the seller anyway and you make sure you have a tracking number from UPS or FedEx (not a USPS delivery confirmation number). The seller still refuses to issue a refund. Now how do you convince PayPal to take another look at your claim?

Once the package has been received by the seller, send an email to appeal@paypal.com and complaint-response@paypal.com. with the basic facts and the tracking number along with the carrier(UPS/FedEx).

This will **not** work if you sent a payment to a hijacked PayPal account. This will only work if you purchased an item that was misrepresented or broken and the seller refused to issue a refund after receiving the return.

You can also call PayPal and talk to someone. Contrary to Internet legend, they do offer phone support.

CHAPTER 6

PHISHING EMAILS

The best way to avoid a train is to see it coming. Scams are the same way. If you know what to look for, you can see them coming a mile away. There may be no flashing lights or gates to stop you from walking into a scam, but you can learn to look both ways before you step in front of the scam train.

Phishing is the act of sending fake emails or using fake websites to trick people into revealing personal information like passwords. The criminals are Fishing for information.

When you enter your user ID and password on eBay or PayPal, make sure you are on the real website. Scammers send out thousands of fake emails, often called spoof or phishing emails, to trick people into going to their fake website which looks exactly like eBay or PayPal. The criminals want to trick people into revealing their passwords.

These look-alike websites may look exactly like eBay or PayPal, and they may even transfer you to the real website after you enter your password, but they are fake. The user ID and passwords are captured by the criminals. You can verify that you are on the real eBay.com website by looking at the address bar of your browser. When you are entering your login information, you should see the security SSL lock and the address should start with https. If it does not start with https then do not enter your user ID or password.

Protect your eBay and PayPal accounts. Never share your password with anyone. Not even family members. If they want to use eBay, let them setup their own accounts. If there is some reason they cannot setup their own account, then you do not want them using yours.

Real site: https://signin.eBay.com/ws/eBayISAPI.dll?SignIn

Make sure when entering your username and password the website always starts with https://

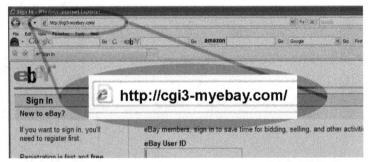

**Fake website that looks like a real eBay login page. This is NOT eBay.
The real login page will always start with https:// never http://**

Fake site: http://signin.ebay.com.klvu.voilieves.kr/ws/signin.php
Fake site: http://secure.ebay-site1.com/ebay.com/login.php
Fake site: http://ebay.com.secure.jkslfkkd.cn/eBayISAPI.dll.SignIn
Fake site: http://cgi3-ebay.com/login.php

All fake sites start with http:// and not the correct https://
Fake sites are only easy to spot if you look at the address URL. If you do enter your password into a fake site, it may transfer to the real website, it may continue and ask for additional personal information, or it may give a fake error message claiming the system is down.

This is the real eBay login page. NEVER enter your eBay or PayPal password into any website that does not show BOTH https:// at the start of the address and the SSL padlock. Use the free MyLittleMole.com toolbar to identify spoof sites automatically.

Criminals use any email they think will trick the recipient into clicking on a link.

Examples of Phishing emails:

"We were updating our accounts and found missing information in your profile..."
"Your account must be updated or it will be disabled..."
"During a regular security check we found a problem with your account..."
"You Won! Just login here......."
"This was sent by eBay...Where is my stuff I am reporting you to eBay..."
"Suspicious activity detected on your PayPal account..."
"You are invited to join the Power Seller Program..."
"Is this other auction selling the same item you have listed"
"Has this auction ripped off your photos?"
"Free Listing Day.. list in the next 24 hours using this link...for free"
"Paypal Terms of service change: ACTION REQUIRED"
"Paypal terms of service violation"
"Paypal Limited Access..."

Criminal emails can be spotted easily because they do not contain your real name. EBay starts all messages with your user ID and real name, not your first name, not your email address, but the name you used to sign up on EBay. PayPal emails always contain the real name you used to create your account and they are sent to the email address used as the primary email address.

This is a real email from eBay. It shows the persons real name AND their eBay ID. It was also sent to the email address John used to register at eBay and not a random or undisclosed-recipients address.

This fake email is easy to spot. It does not contain the persons actual eBay ID AND Name in the first line. It was sent to an email address that this person does not have registered with eBay. The poor grammar is also a tip-off. The link http://signin.ebay.com does not go to eBay, but to a different website.

UNEXPECTED INVITATIONS

Phishers will use any means to trick recipients of their spam into clicking links. One common trick is to send fake "Power Seller Welcome" emails which tell the eBay member they have been accepted into the power seller program, just click the link. The link then goes to a look-alike site the scammer setup. This same technique is used for "Activate your Premiere membership", "You have Won $200", "We will pay you $50 to take this survey", type scams. All of these emails link to fake websites. By far, the most common method is to use an Urgent Plea such as "Account On Hold" or "Account Suspension" type messages.

Fake emails frequently claim your account is going to be suspended, your information needs to be updated, a complaint has been filed, there is a security problem, or it makes some outrageous claim. The criminals want to upset or frighten the reader so they act quickly and click on the link without thinking about it.

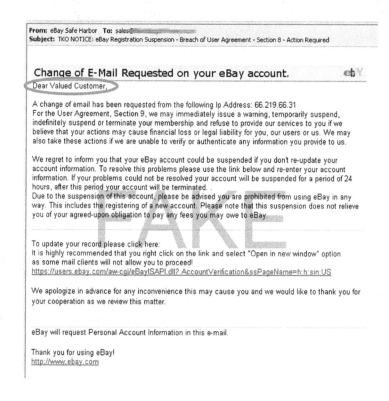

This fake email is easy to spot. It does not contain the persons actual eBay ID AND Name in the first line. Instead it says 'Valued Customer'. Also, this message was sent to an email address that was not registered with eBay. It continues to make an urgent plea attempting to trick the user into clicking on a link. The link shown is NOT the website the user is taken to. The destination is a look-alike fake website. If this user is unsure about the legitimacy of the email, they should go to the real eBay website by typing the URL ebay.com into their browser and login to the real site. Then check their settings and Message Center messages there. They should not click any links in any email.

Seven Warning Signs for Fake Emails

1. Email sent to an email address that is not the one you used for eBay or PayPal registration.
2. The email does not include the member's full real name but instead has a general introduction like Dear eBay User or PayPal Member. All real eBay or PayPal messages will include the full name you used to register.
3. Emails threatening to suspend your account or otherwise demanding urgent action.
4. Emails that contain links to websites other than the https:// pages of eBay or PayPal (You should never click on email links anyway).
5. Bad grammar or misspelled words are common signs of scammers.
6. Email contains links to websites that ask for additional information after login or claim there is a system problem after the password is entered.
7. Forged email headers. This can be difficult to detect unless you are familiar with the raw email header information.

A message with ONE of these signs is most likely a fraudulent email message. Never click on a link in such an email. If you are unsure, go to eBay or PayPal by typing the URL into your browser. If PayPal has a real message for you, it will appear when you login. If eBay has a real message for you it will either appear at login or it will be in your Message Center.

If you fall for one of these and then realize it is fake, go to the real eBay or PayPal sites and change your password. The hacker cannot access your account after you change the password.

The same criminals often send fake PayPal messages. These message look exactly like the real PayPal email. Criminals can use information from expensive eBay auctions to impersonate real sellers too.

This email is really from PayPal. It was received minutes after a transaction occurred. It contains the REAL NAME of the person who owns the PayPal account in the first line. It was sent to the Primary email address the user has registered with PayPal. It also refers to the eBay ID of the account owner.

This email is clearly a fake. It does not contain the REAL NAME of the person to whom it was sent. Hovering the mouse over the link also shows that the destination URL is not the PayPal.com website. Clicking the link goes to a site that does not begin with https://

Fake messages have either no introduction line or they will use a generic introduction like **Dear PayPal Member** or **Attention eBay Member.**

Never click on any link in an email like this. Never click any link in any email ever! Go to https://www.PayPal.com (note the https) and login to your real account directly. If there is any problem, it will be in your message center there or will appear when you login.

An email link does not necessarily go to the location it shows on screen. This email link goes to a fake website. If you were to click on the link you would see it is not an https address so you immediately know this is not the real PayPal website.

Criminals will sometimes send fake complaint emails. These appear to be from eBay or from other eBay users. They may ask a question or claim non-payment or fraud. Their purpose is to either verify that your email address is valid by tricking you into replying, or trick you into clicking on a link to a look-alike eBay or PayPal site.

Fake Complaint Emails are common. Here is a fake email which appears to come from another eBay member. You should always login to your MyMessage console to verify and reply to such messages. Never reply directly and never click on links in emails.

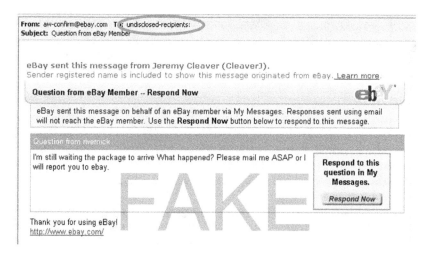

This email is clearly fake. It was not sent to a specific person but to 'Undisclosed-Recipients' which indicates the same email was sent to many people. The introduction says who it is FROM, but it should show the REAL NAME of the person it is TO and their eBay ID. The Respond-Now button links to a fake website which asks for the user's eBay ID and password. The scammer tries to threaten the recipient to make them panic and click on the Respond Now button without thinking.

The purpose of this message is to trick the recipient into clicking on the link which goes to a website the scammer created.

Remember the rule, look for https when you enter your password and only enter your eBay or PayPal ID when you type in the web addresses yourself. Never click a link in an email.

Any email message you receive promising to make money on eBay or promising any service is a scam. If you pay these people money you will be ripped off. No matter how good the offer sounds, or how much money they claim you can make, they are lying. These messages may have links to fake look-alike eBay sites or to other websites claiming to offer eBay related services. No legitimate company will send you an email offering to sell you anything. Email messages from companies you have not purchased anything from or from companies you have never signed up to receive emails from, is spam. Your email address was stolen by these dishonest people and they are also stealing mail services by sending you these fake messages. Spammers cannot be trusted because all spammers are dishonest. They would not send spam if they were legitimate businesses.

```
**************************************************
YOU DON`T HAVE TO BE A GENIUS TO SUCCEED ON EBAY!
**************************************************

Kim from Oklahoma made $500.00 the first time she
tried selling on EBAY!

- She used our Auction Success Kit!

- She earned it in a few short hours!

- She had no past experience!

-       Our Kit is FREE for a limited time, get it
now!

Follow this link:
http://www.conncolsockity.com/efd/
```

This spam email attempts to lure the viewer to a fraudulent website. This website is clearly fraudulent because the URL is nonsense random characters which indicates it is a throw-away site they expect to be disabled because of their illegal activities, they never say who they are, they never give a real website address or real email address, the FROM address is faked, they sent this to a private email address they did not have permission to use, I could go on but you get the idea. They promise a free kit to trick people into clicking the link. Once they have someone at their website, they will try to obtain their credit card number, eBay ID or other information. They may try to lure the reader into a drop-ship scam or other scam. These sites will not ship anything. They are only trying to scam people out of their credit card numbers, eBay login or other information.

Notice how the link is either random nonsense words or gibberish random letters. This is a common tactic of spammers. They will steal a credit card number, then use that to register fake domains like this. By the time the fraud is discovered and the spammer's domain has been shut down, they have collected many more credit card numbers which they will make fraudulent charges to. They may offer something for free to trick people into visiting the website. This may be to verify the email address is valid or they may then offer some other item for a very low price to trick readers into giving out their credit card numbers.

You can never trust anyone who sends an email like this. They may or may not offer the actual product they claim to offer. Most of the time they offer nothing and are only trying to collect credit card numbers, or other personal information

FAKE UNSUBSCRIBE LINKS

Sometimes these spam messages appear to originate from legitimate companies or may offer products you know to be legitimate. Remember, spammers are all criminals. They have no intention of sending you anything. Their only purpose is to obtain your credit card number and personal information. They can pretend to be any company, offer any product at any price. They can copy logos from any company and pretend to be eBay, PayPal, Amazon.com, your local bank, or any company. They never have to ship anything. No legitimate company sends spam. Ignore any email that offers to sell you anything or wants you to go to any website.

The simple rule is, never buy anything from any email you receive. Anyone who sends you an email message trying to sell you something is a criminal. They have already stolen from you. When you pay for Internet service you are paying for the services spammers steal such as system usage, storage space for their spam, bandwidth, and security measures required to guard against spam. They have also illegally used your private email address and used fake information in the return address and likely impersonated another company too. No company should send you any newsletters or solicitations unless you go to their website, enter your email to subscribe, then reply to a confirmation email to confirm you want to receive their messages. If you have not done this for a company, then you have not given them authorization to use your email address for any sales offers.

PRIVATE IS PRIVATE

No one has any reason to ask you for any personal information through eBay's Message Center, by email or by phone. Never give out your home address, social security number, driver's license number, checking account, password, nothing! Many scammers will begin by asking simple questions to make the victim comfortable talking to them. Then they ask for more sensitive information. They may do this by email or after obtaining your phone number by email, they may call you on the phone. No one should ask for this information over the phone. Anyone who calls you on the phone and asks for personal information, a credit card, or social security number is trying to scam you. Anyone can lie about what company they are calling from. Caller ID information can also be faked. No matter how nice they sound, or how confident they are, if they call you and want information or money, it is a SCAM.

CHAPTER 7

CRIMINAL ORGANIZATION

What does anyone gain from these phishing emails? It is much more complicated than simply accessing your PayPal balance. The criminals have a plan and these emails, along with other spam messages, are part of it.

The criminals post fake auctions, redirect the money through stolen or hijacked bank accounts either directly, through hijacked PayPal accounts, or through their fake escrow companies. The money is transferred outside of the US or, the dumber criminals spend it on weekend parties until the authorities catch up with them.

Don't think they are all high school kids looking for some party money either. Some of these scammers are part of large criminal organizations. They run these scams as a business. Some of these scammers, yes, you should know what I am about to say, are tied to terrorist organizations. This is an easy way to obtain funding and it is used just as much as trafficking in stolen goods, drugs, or any other high profit illegal enterprise. Internet fraud is one of the least risky scams they can run.

Anatomy of a Scam

1. Setup look-alike eBay, PayPal or other websites.
2. Send out fake phishing emails to draw people to the fake websites and obtain logins or personal information.
3. Use stolen credit card information to register domains and buy hosting to setup fake websites that look like a payment service or an escrow company.
4. Post fake auctions offering expensive items at bargain prices, again using hijacked eBay accounts and financial information previously obtained.
5. Tell buyers to send payments to hijacked PayPal accounts or by Western Union or through fake escrow company websites at previously setup hosting companies.
6. Continue to scam victims until the account is shut down, then move to the next account.

Who are scammers?

There are different types of scammers and they do things differently.
- Professional Criminals: Some scammers are professional criminals. They may be working on their own or connected to organized crime or even terrorist organizations. They will begin with a plan and hijack accounts or create new accounts to scam people for big money. These criminals are the most difficult for an individual to prosecute because they are mostly outside of the US and hide their tracks. They use fake accounts and hijacked accounts.
- Dishonest Individuals: Sellers who intentionally misrepresent items as new or good condition or working when they are not. Buyers who bid with no intention of paying or who intend to reverse the payment '*just this one time*'. They use their own accounts.
- Small Time Crooks: Small time criminals, looking to make some quick money or sell items they have burglarized locally. They use their own eBay accounts or setup accounts with fake information.
- Fun Scammers: Some scammers are only interested in making enough money to pay for something they want immediately. These are often teenagers who want to pay for a weekend party or want to buy a specific item. They may use their own accounts, parents or friends accounts, or setup new accounts with fake information.

Scammers offer items that appeal to a large number of people. They want to scam many people at once. If they offer a car, a laptop, or some other popular and expensive item, they can scam a lot of money from fewer people. Professional criminals are less likely to offer collectables. Small time crooks who follow a specific area, may try this. Sometimes, a small time criminal will see an expensive collectable and re-list a similar auction weeks later. This does not always work because collectors recognize when an auction is posted to their group with the same photos as a recent auction. Some will see the scam, but others will assume the deal did not go through and the owner is re-auctioning the item.

The crooks may offer a less expensive item if they can list it as Dutch auction with a buy it now price. This allows them to sell and receive payment for many of the items quickly. Professional criminals do not usually scam anyone by offering a $30 collector Star Wars cup. The professional would go for the high priced items or the items they can sell quickly and in large quantities. They prefer laptops, vehicles, counterfeit designer clothing, and other high dollar items.

COMMON SCAMS

WESTERN UNION

Western Union is a fine company that provides a great service for sending payments TO FRIENDS AND FAMILY. This service is not for sending auction payments. Any seller who insists on a Western Union payment is a scammer.

You will see this repeated in countless scams throughout this book. Do not pay for an auction with Western Union. Any seller who asks you to pay by Western Union or who sends you detailed instructions on how to pay by Western Union is a crook. Once you send a Western Union payment, your money is gone and it is not coming back.

Scammers will post auctions for expensive items, then insist on a Western Union payment. When they receive the money, they disappear and ship nothing.

Any buyer who claims they have sent payment to you by Western Union and insists you ship immediately before picking up the payment is a crook. Scammers bid on expensive items, then send fake Western Union look-alike emails to the seller which claim payment has been made, but will only be released when the item is shipped. The email is a fake; this is not how Western Union works. The bidder will receive the goods and the seller will never receive any payment.

Just because a buyer or seller offers to use Western Union as a payment option does not make them a crook. If they insist on it as the only payment method and will not accept other legitimate payment methods, they are a scammer.

Many sellers realized they were about to be scammed before shipping. Now scammers send a second email that also appears to be from Western Union asking for personal information or asking them to register at a website. The website is a fake look-alike site setup by the scammer to con the victim out of their personal and financial information. Even if the seller realizes the sale is not real, they may reveal their personal information first. The scammer then uses this information to commit other fraud. This scam is also used for other payment services so beware of any emails claiming you have receive a payment which tell you to **go ahead and ship the goods**. Verify at the company's real website first.
Beware of any seller who states in the auction or by email:

"The transaction will be made thru Western Union with the ebay protection."

This is a guarantee the seller is a scammer. Western Union has no eBay protection. EBay says specifically not to use Western Union. Western Union says specifically not to use their service to pay for auctions.

ke auction or modified auction scams are posted by criminals who steal other people's
ay passwords using the phishing emails and look-alike websites previously discussed.
ey obtain someone's user id and password, then post fake, high priced items for sale
modify existing listings by the seller with a fake contact address and an offer to sell
a fixed price. Buyers think they are contacting the account owner, but are contacting
thief. When they send a money order or other payment, it goes to the crook. Make
re you are contacting the real account owner and if it sounds too good to be true, it is.

Tᴏᴏ Gᴏᴏᴅ Tᴏ Bᴇ Tʀᴜᴇ

Be careful of anything that seems too good to be true. eBay is a popular marketplace
which makes it a favorite hangout for scammers. They are usually easy to avoid with
some common sense. Some bend the truth and some outright lie about what they are
selling.

If someone has a $10,000.00 motorcycle and they are selling it on eBay for $3,000, ask yourself, why did their neighbor not buy it? If My neighbor had a $10,000 motorcycle, I would gladly buy it for $3,000 cash and then sell it on eBay for $9,000 myself.

Any deal that seems too good to be true IS TOO GOOD TO BE TRUE. It is a scam, a rip-off, a crime in the making. I don't know how to make it any clearer. No one is going to sell you something for half its value.

Beware of anyone offering an item at an unrealistic discount.

Rᴇᴘᴏʀᴛ Tʜɪs Lɪsᴛɪɴɢ Sᴄᴀᴍ

Scammers sometimes use auction listings themselves to steal eBay user ID's and passwords. This is similar to the phishing emails scam. The scammer posts a fake auction that is clearly inappropriate or pornographic. At the top or bottom they add links that appear to be eBay links, but actually go to a webpage setup by the scammer. The link redirects the user to a login page where they are requested to enter their eBay login and password. This is a fake page on a website created by the scammer and not the real eBay site. When the user enters their information, it goes straight to the criminal. The criminal can now hijack the well meaning user's account for other scams. Make sure you only enter your eBay ID on https SSL pages that are on the real eBay website. You should only click on the Report This Auction link at the very bottom of the auction page or in the header(depending on which page version you are viewing) and do not click links that are part of the description.

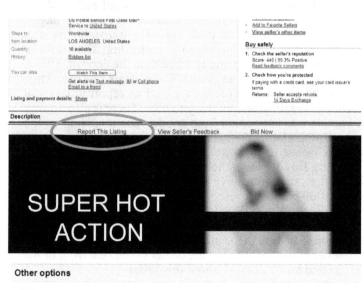

Inappropriate auctions in the main categories may have fake 'Report This Listing' links which go to a page that asks for your eBay password. Notice that the above Report link is inside the description. The real link is at the bottom of the auction page under Other Options.

41

This auction was posted by someone who has not previously sold vehicles and has sold nothing for six months, yet the listing looks professional and contains over 20 photos and lots of details. The actual listing continued for several pages. The terms demand a $500 non-refundable deposit by wire transfer. The non refundable deposits is what this scammer is interested in collecting. They offer to split a warranty payback which is not coincidentally more than the deposit. This is unusual. Why give money away? Beware of any *complicated* deals like this. They also post a CarFax report in the auction. Never trust a CarFax report unless you obtain it from the CarFax site yourself. These are easy to fake. There is also no way to verify the VIN in the auction was not copied from another auction. None of the photos showed a VIN. The listing claims the item is listed locally and the auction may be ended early. This is meant to pressure those interested into contacting the seller immediately or using Buy It Now. The seller has a Buy It Now price of $8,990.00 but in the listing they say the reserve is $10,100. Why would they set the Buy It Now price over $1000 below the reserve price? The BIN price is $2000 below blue book price according to Kelly Blue Book kbb.com

Is this a fake? It looks too good to be true to me and there are inconsistencies. They do list a dealer's phone number in the auction, but the dealer could be a front or the dealer may have the real car and know nothing about this seller.

ROLEX AND JEWELRY SCAMS

The scams that work by mail work even better on the Internet. The counterfeit Rolex, or any expensive jewelry, scam is common in spam and on eBay. No one sells a new watch worth $1000 for $400. If the buyer receives anything, it will be a $10 counterfeit watch or other cheap jewelry.

Jewelry scams also include offering zircons as real diamonds, synthetic stones as real, and offering plated gold as solid gold. Dishonest sellers depend on buyers not knowing the difference and many buyers cannot tell they have been scammed even when they receive the item.

Jewelry appraisals are worthless. Jewelers inflate prices on jewelry by 1000% or more. Jewerly items purchased wholesale for $30 commonly sell retail for $300. Purchasing a piece of jewelry for $200 with a *genuine appraisal* of $500 means you have a $50 piece of jewelry if you are lucky. A $5 piece of costume jewelry if you are not.

WAIT A LITTLE LONGER

Dishonest sellers sometimes use the '*wait a little longer*' technique to put off buyers they have scammed. They may apologize and say they will send a refund, but not immediately. They may say the item will ship in a week or two weeks when it is already a week past due. This is a common tactic to delay complaints. If the scammer can delay complaints until they can transfer the money out of their PayPal account and disappear, they can get away with a lot of money plus scam more buyers. Don't fall for this new version of '*it's in the mail*' type scam. If the seller cannot provide a tracking number or the item is past due(usually ten days to two weeks since payment was sent) file for a PayPal refund. Do not cancel the PayPal complaint until you have the item.

SHILL BIDDING

Shill bidding generally means bidding with no intent to buy. Shill bidding occurs when a seller bids on their own items, or has an accomplice bid for them, for the purpose of running up the bid amount. This is a violation of eBay rules. Dishonest sellers may setup alternate eBay accounts to bid on their own auctions or they may ask for the assistance of a friend who can bid on their items. The high bidder is not required to pay for the auction if they should accidentally win. Some scammers use private auction formats to hide shill bidding. There are a number of variations to shill bidding.

Shill-Valuation
Sellers attempt to inflate the value of an item by posting a fixed price auction at a high price, then buying their own item using a shill account. This is not in violation of eBay rules since it is not technically shill bidding. They then relist the item for auction and either hope buyers will check past auctions and see the high value, or state in their auction to check past auctions and give a link. Potential bidders see the high price when they check past auctions. This effectively gives a false valuation to the item. A variation of this type of auction occurs when the seller posts the item using their shill account, then buys the item using another account or their seller account. If the auction is private, no one can see who the high bidder is. If the auction is not private, then everyone can see that the current seller was the high bidder(if the user ID is not hidden by eBay for

high value auctions). The seller may even claim they recently purchased the item on eBay which makes potential bidders think they purchased the item being offered at the previous auction's high price when in fact the seller had the item all along. This type of auction can be difficult to identify. Look closely at the bid history and buying history of the buyer and seller of the previous and current auctions. See if they have a habit of bidding on each other's auctions. Look at the wording and layout of the previous auction. Does the grammar, look-and-feel, of the auction appear similar to the newly listed auction? Maybe the same seller is behind both of them. Is the suspect shill account a low feedback or zero feedback member? Why would a low feedback member offer an expensive item and why would the current seller buy the item at a fixed price from a seller with no history? Was the suspected shill buyer account created the same day as the first auction listing? These tip-offs can identify Shill-Valuation deceit.

Shill-Frenzy

These auctions occur when sellers use shill bidding to artificially inflate prices and create the appearance of interest in an item. They effectively manufacture competition. If you have ever attended a live auction, you know when an item starts slow and suddenly several furious bids, it will bring other bidders into the bidding frenzy. This is the same effect sellers want to create with their auctions. They will start with a low opening bid and using two or more shill accounts, they will bid back and forth raising prices. Shill-Frenzy bidding can also be difficult to identify. Are the two bidders running up the price simply inexperienced or are they alter egos of the seller? Look at their bidding pattern, does it make sense? Are they bidding $5 increments back and forth? It is unusual for both parties to be bidding in the same increments or in round number amounts($20 and not $20.05). Are the bids in clusters? Does one bidder bid, then a couple of minutes later another, then the first again. Then the next day the process is repeated at the same time of day? That looks like the seller is logging in at the same time and bidding up the price a little each day. Shill-Frenzy bids are usually placed in the early days of an auction to create a fake frenzy of bidding interest.

Shill-Reserve

Shill-Reserve auctions occur when sellers place one high shill bid. This is effectively the same as a reserve price except there is no notation by the item. Both reserve and shill-reserve auctions have a secret price associated with them. The seller does not have to sell the item to a real bidder unless another bidder exceeds the shill-reserve. If a seller has an item they do not want to sell for less than $200, they may list the item for $1 opening bid and then place a shill bid using a second account for $200. Any real bidder who places a bid is automatically outbid until they cross the $200 level. Reserve price auctions are basically shill-reserve auctions except they are allowed by eBay rules. These auctions can be identified by checking the past sales history of the seller and of the specific item. If the seller keeps relisting the same item and the same bidder keeps winning, that is a sure sign of shill bidding. If it were a non-paying bidder, the seller would block them from future auctions and not allow them to continue bidding. The bidder may be an alter ego of the seller if the same bidder keeps placing single bids on high priced auctions of the seller, but rarely wins or won items are relisted. If a bidder bids once on more than one auction and always bids in round numbers, it may be a shill account. Shill accounts frequently have zero feedback or one feedback from the seller. The sellers use them only for shill bidding and never build legitimate feedback. Shill-Reserve sellers often set round numbers, like $100 as their shill-reserve. Real bidders would bid a non round number such as $101.05. Shill-Reserve bids are usually placed early in an auction by shill accounts with low or no feedback. They are often the first or second bids placed.

Shill-Buyers

Shill bidding is not exclusive to seller fraud. Buyers can use the same technique to commit fraud. Instead of using Shill Bidding to run up the price, dishonest bidders can use Shill Bidding to drive down the price. A buyer sees an expensive item they want to bid on. They put in a high bid. More than the item is worth. Then with a second shill account, or an accomplice, they place a second bid higher than the previous bid. Now the item has a high bid that is above the value of the item. During the time of the auction no one else can bid because the price is far above the item's value. Just before the auction ends, the second bidder withdraws their bid leaving the first bidder at the opening bid amount. This bidder has effectively eliminated any competitors for most of the auction. There will be no watchers of the auction because no one is interested in bidding higher than the highest bid. There may be a few last minute bidders, but the dishonest bidder can obtain a bargain because they have effectively changed a 7 day auction, into an auction only a few hours long. Other bidders were locked out for most of the auction duration. Beware of any bidder who retracts a high bid near the end of the auction leaving another bidder as high bidder. If possible, the auction should be cancelled and re-listed or reported to eBay. This technique is also called **Bid-Shielding**. The second bidder, shields the first bidder to prevent anyone else from bidding against the first bidder.

Bid-Shielding or Shill-Buyers can use the technique on Mystery Envelope auctions or Emotional Plea auctions that offer a bonus to anyone bidding a certain amount. The bidders will bid so that the threshold is crossed and then request their bonus money. If they are paid, they will retract their bids. This is an example of a scammer scamming another scammer.

TRACKING BID SHIELDING

Bid Shielding or Shill Bidders can be a nightmare for a seller. The seller believes they have a really good bid and then 12 hours before the end of the auction, it is retracted leaving a very low bid.

If you believe your auction is receiving fraudulent high bids, check the buyer's bid history. Under Advanced Search, search for the persons User ID and select the option to see all auctions they have bid on. Do they have a history of retracting bids? What about the second high bidder who is now high bidder? Do they have a similar pattern of bidding on the same auctions?

If you are the seller and you see Bid-Shielding, cancel the auction immediately. If necessary, contact eBay and have it cancelled. You should never sell an item or allow the auction to close if a bidder retracts a bid close to the final 12 hours of the auction. Something is wrong if they do. Bidders are not supposed to retract bids within the final 12 hours of the auction, but if they select "Cannot Contact Seller" as the reason, they will be allowed to retract their bid even in the final 12 hours. If anyone retracts a bid within the last 12 hours of your auction, you can be assured there is a scam in the works.

To spot Shill Bidders look for:

1. A bidder who joined recently and who only bids on auctions from the same seller.
2. A bidder with the same location as the seller or who hides their true location by using a location like "United States."
3. A bidder who sells items similar to the seller and whose auctions look similar.
4. A bidder who bids repeatedly throughout the auction and bids in small increments or round numbers.
5. A bidder who bids in a pattern, such as every day at 2 PM.
6. A bidder who has bid on the same item from the same seller in the past or who is bidding or has bid on the same item in other current auctions.
7. A bidder who won the item from this or another seller already in the past.
8. A bidder who bids when bidding from others "slows down".

GIFT CERTIFICATE SCAM

A scam seller can offer a gift certificate with an interesting tale of how it was acquired for pennies on the dollar. The gift certificate is only good at one site you never heard of before, which is either overpriced or uses excessive shipping charges. If you have not figured it out yet, the seller of the gift certificate is the owner of the website. A $1000 gift certificate may also have small print that requires a $10,000 purchase to redeem it. A $20 gift certificate may require a $100 purchase of items that are already double retail price.

Another scam is to offer seemingly expensive items that are in fact cheap junk through these sites. Gold chains that are plated or painted or counterfeit designer items that the seller can no longer sell on eBay.

YES?????? THE ITEM IS GREAT????

Beware of any auction with lots of question marks. This usually indicates the person who posted the auction did so from a computer that was setup for a foreign language like Chinese or Korean. Those characters do not normally display and will show up as question marks instead. If the seller claims to be in the US and you see ?? in unusual places or foreign characters, then he is not in the US. Some scammers simply use excessive question marks. Any auction with lots of question marks should be regarded as fraudulent especially if the seller claims to be in the USA or an English speaking country. Normal, people simply do not use punctuation this way.

THREE MONKEYS AUCTION (UNKNOWN OR SURPRISE BOX)

You remember the three proverbial monkeys, hear no evil, see no evil, speak no evil. A three monkeys auction is for an unknown item, an unknown collection of items, or a surprise box. The seller pretends they cannot see or hear or speak the contents.

The Unknown item or Mystery Item auction is for an item that the seller claims they are unfamiliar with.

For this scam, the scammer does not need an auction ID that has a feedback history. They can pretend to be a new and inexperienced member by claiming they don't know what the item is. This leads bidders to believe they can take advantage of the inexperienced seller. Buyers are less likely to complain or post negative feedback when they act out of devious motives. The buyer does not want to reveal that they attempted to take advantage of an inexperienced seller or reveal that they were duped. The victim(the buyer) keeps quiet. This gives the dishonest seller an advantage and allows them to run such auctions longer before they are shut down.

Honest sellers sell items in a LOT, dishonest sellers sell items in a Mystery Box.

The seller may claim the items were received as an inheritance, purchased from a yard sale, found in the attic, or some other means that would explain why the seller is not familiar with the item.

I just inherited my uncles stamp collection and I am selling
it off. I have no idea what these are but here are four for sale.

This designer handbag was a gift from my great aunt.
She was very wealthy so I am sure it is an original.

An alternative to the Unknown auction is the Miscellaneous Lot. The seller will show an unclear photo of several items that appears to show several worthless items and one valuable item. The seller may offer several 'unknown' or 'unchecked' condition vinyl LP's. A collector recognizes the sleeve artwork of one as a known valuable record. When the buyer receives the record set, the sleeve of the rare LP contains a different record that is worthless. This is similar to bait-and-switch except the seller can now claim they are innocent of wrongdoing because they never said the item was valuable.

The item can also be counterfeit (fake Tiffany lamp), it could be a photocopy or a printout (not really that rare 1920's political rally handout, but a copy).

Beware of seller ignorance. Serious sellers rarely post items as 'unknown' or 'unchecked'. When the seller takes the position of the three monkeys, he pretends he does not know what the item is to avoid liability or blame when it is revealed as a sham or fake. The seller puts all the risk on the buyer.

You can test the seller by contacting them through eBay and telling them what the item is. This is risky. If the seller is honest, they may cancel the auction or change the opening bid to a higher value. They may also post your comment in the auction for others to see. Dishonest sellers will not reply or will otherwise not act to correct the auction. You can be sure that a seller who really has an expensive item will want potential bidders to know it is valuable.

EVENT TICKETS

You need tickets to that sold out boxing match or ballet and you need them right away. Price is no object. You will pay $200 for tickets that sold for $20 at the box office. You find a seller offering to overnight the tickets and use a Buy-It-Now price. The tickets are overnighted and you leave positive feedback for the seller. When you proudly hand the tickets to the ticket taker, they look at you in a funny way and you notice your tickets do not look like the other tickets people have handed in. Tickets are easy to counterfeit when the buyer does not know what the real ticket looks like. Tickets are great for scammers because they cost nothing to make, the buyers need them urgently, and they sell for high prices. Hijacked accounts with good feedback can be used to sell several tickets which means no work for the criminal if they ship nothing. This is not an especially common scam. It is an occasional scam that is targeted at big events where tickets go for high prices. This scam is usually committed by small time criminals and teenagers looking for some fast cash.

Also beware of anyone selling tickets who is within driving distance but refuses to complete the transaction in person by either letting you pick the tickets up or meeting you somewhere. When you buy tickets it is usually for a local event. If the person claims to be local but will not make the exchange in person, then they are either not local and are only pretending to be local(in which case they do not have the tickets) or they do not have any tickets and it is a scam.

MYSTERY BOX

The mystery or surprise box is always a scam if it is supposed to be valuable. Sometimes sellers will offer hard to sell items like clothes in surprise boxes. It is never worth the amount paid. The seller can manipulate its contents to make sure it is never a bargain.

Some liquidators will offer mystery boxes and include junk they cannot sell. These are broken, have missing parts, are obsolete items, cellphone cases for long discontinued models, pager clips, wrist straps, non working cellphones and dead cellphone batteries. A mystery box may contain the inner tube from a bike tire, a charger for a cordless screwdriver(no screwdriver) and anything else that was left over from this seller's yard sale. A mystery box can also be empty. Mystery boxes are usually full of junk.

Another scam is the '*my roommate moved out and I am selling his stuff*" mystery box auction. Does it make any sense that someone would sell a box of another persons belongings without going through it to check for valuable items?

Dishonest mystery auctions sometimes give a percentage of their winning price to a charity. They do this to make their auction appear legitimate because the charity offer is part of an eBay program that automatically sends a percentage of the money to charity. The problem is that the rest of the money was scammed from the buyer because mystery auctions are all frauds. The fact that part was given to charity makes the buyer less likely to pursue a refund or file a Paypal chargeback which is something the dishonest seller is depending on. All mystery auctions are dishonest but ones that try to use the good name of a charity to conduct their scams are the worst.

No one will every sell you something valuable for less than it is worth.

BIDDER BONUS

A bonus is a payment to the second high bidder or to a bidder who crosses a certain price level. This is supposedly to drive up the bidding, but this is also not an eBay approved sale. The seller has no obligation to the second high bidder. Why would the seller pay someone a bonus for pushing up the price? Maybe the seller is planning to be the second high bidder. This technique also brings out fake bidders. People who have no intention of buying the item but are only bidding to obtain the bonus.

Sellers who offer prizes or bonuses are running contests, not auctions. Beware of any auction that promises "*I will pay a $20 bonus to the bidder who reaches the $275 bid mark*". The seller is running a scam.

MYSTERY ENVELOPE

Mystery envelopes are similar to Mystery Boxes except they are usually for cash or coupons. These are illegal Lotteries or Gambling Schemes.

Sellers sometimes use shill feedback in their own profiles that appears to be from winners.

(+) This guy is great, I won $3000 in my mystery envelope - fraudebayuser(1)

Any feedback claiming someone won big is fraudulent. The seller created a fake account and left themselves feedback.

There are no winners. Why would a seller offering a mystery envelope send someone $1000 in cash for a $10 purchase? This is obviously too good to be true.

Some scammers offering mystery envelopes write a good story and brag about all the cash they have to give away. Some claim they just won thousands at a casino or received an inheritance. If you received a $20,000 inheritance, would you give it away on eBay?

The people who bid on these auctions receive $0.25 to a few dollars, usually ten percent of whatever they paid for the auction.

Mystery Envelopes are a veiled lottery scheme where no one wins. These are illegal. They violate the law as well as PayPal policies.

MULTIPLE UNIQUE ITEMS

Has the seller offered the same unique item in past auctions with the same photo? If a seller offers a '*rare handmade samurai sword*' and shows photos of a clearly aged antique sword, but they keep running the same auction and selling it every few days, it is clear they are not actually selling the sword shown in the auction or the seller is selling cheap reproductions. Check their feedback. You may find they have complaints about shipping an item different from the one in the auction or non delivery.

FAKE LINKS

Scammers in the mystery box groups post fake links to trick people into adding their auction to the viewer's favorites list. When a scammer gets his auction onto many people's favorites list, it makes the auction appear on the popular and pulse listings which gains the dishonest seller more viewers. These sellers sometimes have click here links with fake offers, they show what looks like a video player with an alluring image but it is actually a static image and when the viewer tries to click the play button they are actually clicking a link that adds the item to their favorites even if they did not want to monitor the auction. The use of fake links and fake video images shows how dishonest mystery box/envelope sellers are.

UNTESTED FRAUD

When a seller states '*I didn't test it*' they usually mean '*it does not work, but I don't want to admit it*'. If the item cannot be tested then they may be honest in their description. If the item could be tested, like a CD player, and they did not test it, you must ask why not? This can be a warning sign about the seller, but if you accept that the item is not working, and bid accordingly, you can still come out with a good item you can repair or use for parts.

This is not a scam used by professional criminals. The mildly dishonest person will '*bend the truth*' for this scam. Sellers may not be able to test all items, but any items that can be tested, should be tested.

An exception to this rule is antique electronics. It is never a good idea to test antique electronic equipment, like tube radios, or electro-mechanical antiques by plugging them in. This can cause serious damage. These items must be restored or at least inspected by an expert before power is applied. An exposed wire, dried out capacitor, or loose washer can cause severe damage if the item is plugged in without an inspection.

L33t 5p34k (Leet Speak)

Never buy from any seller who substituted zeros for o's or uses 3's for E's. This is a clear warning sign that the seller cannot be trusted. The only people who use this Leet Speak are spammers and 12 year old wanna-be hackers. Honest sellers do not use Leet Speak. Leet Speak can be used to conceal keywords that the seller is afraid will raise a red flag at eBay security such as i113gal instead of illegal.

SHIPPING TO BE DETERMINED

Never trust a seller who says shipping charges will be determined at auction close. This means if the close price is not high enough, the seller will pad it out with excessive shipping. If the buyer does not want to pay the excessive shipping, the seller will cancel the sale. It is like a reserve price without saying there is a reserve price.

eBook Resale Rights Scam

A common scam on eBay is the offer of an ebook collection with resale rights. These appeal to people wanting to start their own business and offer ebooks for sale. It sounds like a great deal. Buy their collection of ebooks and sell some of them for a few dollars as a download. Unfortunately, this is too good to be true. The eBook collections being sold are mostly stolen material. The sellers do not have the right to sell the books and they certainly do not have the resale rights for them. The buyer does not know this until they have purchased and received the ebook collection. Many of these ebooks are files downloaded from the Internet, recipes that are incomplete, and even saved webpages which clearly have copyright notices on them and state they are not to be copied.

Some of these sellers actually send a webpage of links to websites with free downloadable ebooks and give you the rights to resell their webpage of links. The actual content of the websites is not being sold. Many of the links in these lists go to dead websites. The list is worthless and no honest person can resell it in good conscience.

You may see individual ebooks being offered with *'full resale rights'* This means the author cannot sell the book based on its content so they are giving away resale rights. If the book was good, they would not be doing this because they would be creating competition for themselves.

No one will ever make money selling eBooks for $0.99 each. The listing with Gallery image and PayPal fees will make the net profit six cents.

Don't fall for the *'Buy My eBook Collection With Full Resale Rights'*' scam. There are legitimate ebook sellers on eBay, but they will not offer resale rights to their books. Write your own book; don't buy resale rights to a book no one else wants.

PayPal Intangibles

If a buyer selects 'goods' as the type of purchase during checkout and you are selling an intangible item, you have zero protection from reversals. PayPal only offers protection for tangible, physical goods. Payments for services, downloadable eBooks, airline tickets, or digital content are not covered by their protection program. If you sell a service and the buyer files a reversal, you have no recourse. Instead sell a coupon for your service or similar tangible item and send that to the user as well as sending the digital content. This gives you proof of delivery and seller protection.

One Day Listing Fraud

Beware of one day listings. One day listings are sometimes for items that are not allowed on eBay. Sellers want the listing to close or end with Buy-It-Now before eBay can cancel the auction. These are often posted Friday afternoon with the hope that eBay will not have a chance to review them until Monday. One day auctions are often used by scammers hoping to collect money using a stolen PayPal account or by mail or Western Union and have no intention of shipping any items. Be wary of one day auctions. Legitimate sellers will list items for a longer period to obtain higher bids.

Beware of any auction that makes an emotional plea or tries to play on your sympathy. These are always scams. This is a real title from one of these scammers:

My little Boy Caleb!He Needs Your Help!Come take a look

The scammer then posts photos of their perfectly healthy child, or images of someone else's child they stole from a webpage and claim the child has some specific disease or ailment. They always give plenty of details which came from a medical website.

Auctions that attempt to raise money for unverified charities, or for individuals with hard-luck stories are fraudulent. Auctions are for selling items. Anyone who tries to sell a '*save my child*' story and offers a token item, is running a scam auction.

The hard-luck story is a scam 100% of the time. Psychologically normal people who are having hard times will never post about it in an auction like this.

Please Help, I lost my job, my wife is sick and the bank just foreclosed, buy my mystery box and win a prize.

Beware of sellers who update their auctions with price points. It is not normal for a seller to repeatedly add to their auction listing offering thanks to bidders for reaching a price level and encouraging higher bids. That is the pattern of a snake oil salesman, not an auction.

Thanks so much to all of you, you really warm my heart.
Also lookin for bid mark $275!
The person to hit $275 will get a $20 PayPal gift!

This is clearly a scam. This seller was selling some type of box. It was unclear exactly what you were bidding on from the auction because the description went on and on about their sick child. If they need money then why are they giving out bonuses for bid marks?

Honest sellers never need to tell you a story about how tough they have it. Honest sellers lay out the facts and let the item sell, not their story.

Another emotional appeal is the "*I found a Super Sale*" scam. Instead of pulling at heart strings, this scam appeals to excitement.

I was at XYZ store and they were closing out some open box Gucci handbags, normally $200, a one day sale for $10

Now they are sharing the excitement with everyone. Unfortunately there was no such sale and the items are either non-existent or counterfeit.

I am selling my Gucci handbag for $10 because it was a present from my lousy ex-husband and I want to get rid of it.

Divorce and death are common emotional auction scams. The seller tries to motivate bidders to take advantage of them using their emotional state to justify a low price or to push up prices for items that are not valuable or non existent.

I have even seen scammers claim they are selling cars because their son was killed in a drunk driving accident. It was a lie to lower the defenses of potential buyers who would think they were helping out someone in distress and getting a good deal. It was nothing but a ploy to steal the victim's money. There was no son and no drunk driving accident.

Any seller who depends on an emotional plea is pulling a scam. Only crooked sellers resort to such lies. Honest sellers stick to the facts.

ESTABLISHED ONLINE BUSINESS SCAM

No one will sell an established online business that is making money. Period, never, not going to happen. If you had a business making $1000 per day, would you sell it for $200? If you had a business making $100 a week would you sell it for $200?

These scammers usually lure in victims by stating how much money they are making per month. They claim to make $5,000.00 per month, and are willing to sell for $5,000 but the opening bid is $1. Then they say the business can be run in your spare time or on weekends. If you had a $5,000/month business that you could run in your spare time, would you sell it for $20, $1,000, $5,000? $20,000? No one would.

These auctions are usually careful to say they do not have the time, or they are moving on to bigger projects. They punctuate their claim by saying "my loss is your gain". If the business can be run in someone's spare time, then how do they no longer have the time? Why do they not hire someone to come in once a week to run it for them? Some claim they need money for new projects, but they are offering to sell for less than they would make in one month, often less than they claim they would make in one day.

Some of these sellers routinely sell the same business or various businesses every month. It is very easy. They take a web template, fill in the information, make a fake PayPal payment page and claim they are making a fortune when they have in fact not made one sale.

Some of the sellers offer very low priced established businesses, but then require the buyer to pay an additional $50 or more 'installation fee' above the auction price and the buyer has to host the website on a specific hosting service which is actually owned by the seller. The buyer is not receiving an established business for $20. They are buying a $20/month lifetime webhosting expense. Any auction that offers a 'monthly payment' or 'pay in advance' is not selling a site, they are selling a subscription.

If the seller of a website requires that you become a hosting customer on a specific service(which is their service) and you decide to move to a new hosting service, what happens to the domain name? Ahh, you find out that you bought the website and not the domain. If by some fluke you should buy the website and turn it into a legitimate profitable business, you cannot transfer it because the scammer owns the domain name. The scam seller has total control over your domain, they can monitor your sales, customers, credit card purchases,

STOLEN PROPERTY

EBay is a favorite place for criminals to unload stolen property. It is private and items are not re-sold at local pawn shops where police may look. If you have been burglarized and any of your items can be identified, such as a specific brand of expensive watch or camera, setup a favorites-search on eBay for the item. It may show up. If you suspect an item up for auction may be stolen, check the seller's other auctions and sales history. Look for a member offering an unusual collection of items like DVD players, jewelry, cameras, laptops, or a similar strange mix. It is not unusual for people to sell these items. It is unusual for them to sell just these items, all at once, over and over.

Have you purchased a telephone or answering machine through eBay with months worth of Caller ID info and messages on it? Have you purchased a video camera or still camera with a tape, undeveloped film, or memory card in it that had family photos? No one sells a camera full of photos.

If you purchased an expensive camera, with a storage bag, lens cleaner wipes, extra lenses, extra memory card and when you receive it, you notice it looks like it came from someone's closet, it is stolen. People upgrade their camera and keep the accessories. They do not sell everything in the case along with lens cleaners and filters like this. Someone's house was burglarized and the thief grabbed their full camera bag to sell on eBay.

If your home is ever burglarized, check out eBay and Craigslist.org carefully for the next few weeks. You may find some of your items appearing on those sites.

UNCLEAR PRICING

Beware of sellers who cannot give a firm price. If a seller has one price in the buy it now area or auction area, then in the auction he list s four or five different shipping costs, then charges sales tax, then charges insurance, then charges handling, then lists a different cost for shipping, this is a seller to avoid. The seller is trying to artificially increase the price without the buyer noticing. The seller should lump all of these costs into one price which is shipping & handling. I have seen sellers offer an inexpensive product and in the description say shipping was $3 then in the terms claim shipping was $4.55, then later in the terms say there was a handling charge of $1.50. Any seller who tries to split shipping/insurance/tax into categories or tries to invent additional tack on charges, or lists conflicting shipping amounts should not be trusted. This is an attempt to overcharge and confuse the buyer or it is a listing by a completely incompetent seller.

ADULT AUCTION SCAMS

The Adult Area tends to attract the small time criminal including teenagers looking for some quick money. These scammers will list expensive items for sale at well below the retail or market costs. The feedback of the sellers is usually very low and they may even have negatives from previous sales. The attraction of the Adult Area for scammers is the ability to get payment by money order. Many buyers in the adult area do not want to use PayPal or credit cad. The buyer is much less likely to complain if he purchased a naughty item. Once the scammer has the money, he simply never ships because he never had the item in the first place. Beware of super bargains from low feedback sellers in the Adult Section or any other category.

ESTABLISHED ONLINE BUSINESS SCAM

No one will sell an established online business that is making money. Period, never, not going to happen. If you had a business making $1000 per day, would you sell it for $200?

These scammers usually lure in victims by stating how much money they are making per month. They claim to make $5,000.00 per month, and are willing to sell for $5,000 but the opening bid is $1. Then they say the business can be run in your spare time or on weekends. If you had a $5,000/month business that you could run in your spare time, would you sell it for $20, $1,000, $5,000? $20,000? No one would.

These auctions are usually careful to say they do not have the time, or they are moving on to bigger projects. They punctuate their claim by saying "my loss is your gain". If the business can be run in someone's spare time, then how do they no longer have the time? Why do they not hire someone to come in once a week to run it for them? Some claim they need money for new projects, but they are offering to sell for less than they would make in one month, often less than they claim they would make in one day.

Some of these sellers routinely sell the same business or various businesses every month. It is very easy. They take a web template, fill in the information, make a fake PayPal payment page and claim they are making a fortune when they have in fact not made one sale.

Some of the sellers offer very low priced established businesses, but then require the buyer to pay an additional $50 or more 'installation fee' above the auction price and the buyer has to host the website on a specific hosting service which is actually owned by the seller. The buyer is not receiving an established business for $20. They are buying a $20/month lifetime webhosting expense. Any auction that offers a 'monthly payment' or 'pay in advance' is not selling a site, they are selling a subscription.

If the seller of a website requires that you become a hosting customer on a specific service(which is their service) and you decide to move to a new hosting service, what happens to the domain name? Ahh, you find out that you bought the website and not the domain. If by some fluke you should buy the website and turn it into a legitimate profitable business, you cannot transfer it because the scammer owns the domain name. The scam seller has total control over your domain, they can monitor your sales, customers, credit card purchases, everything. The scammer can change your passwords and redirect payments to their own PayPal or credit card accounts taking your business away from you.

In the fine print they claim '*no refunds and no guarantees*' after they have already claimed $5000/month income. If they make any reference to drop shippers, that is a sure sign of a scam. The drop-shipper may actually be the person selling the site.

When looking at a business, you have to examine the profit margin. Not just the gross income or the 'earnings potential' whatever that is. If you can make $250 per day, what does that actually cost you for the product and shipping, advertising, the website, and other services? If your expenses are $260 per day, it is not a very good business. This analysis does not really matter because no one is going to sell you a business that is making money through eBay anyway.

Beware of proof of income screenshots. Most, I think it is safe to say all of the PayPal or other screenshots are fakes. This is outright fraud, but it can be hard to prove. You cannot see the persons PayPal account for yourself. Check the seller's past auctions. They may use the same information, the same 'proof' of income for other domains and other websites.

Many of these websites offer a proof of income that shows payments of $200 or more per payment, but the description says the site sells $14.95/month subscriptions. So, why are people paying $200+ dollars per transaction? Why do these 'proof of income' pages not show a number of $14.95 charges? These only prove the listings are scams.

Beware of any claims saying a website generated thousands of dollars in days. Any new website that generates thousands of dollars may be a scam that is advertised through spam. You do not want a legitimate looking site that has just scammed thousands of people out of their money.

Any seller who wants Western Union for a website is a guaranteed scammer.

A variation on this scam is the "Established Web Site Scam"

These sellers offer the same web sites over and over. They simply register new domain names and change the name of the site. They may not claim they are profitable businesses. In the small print they redefine Established to mean the domain is registered. The big print is where it says "ESTABLISHED ".

Do a Google search to see if the website actually exists. Pick a phrase from it and search with quotes around the phrase. This should make the site come to the top. Search again for general terms and see how high the site appears in the listings.

If the seller gives some odd keywords to search on to show the ranking of the site don't believe it. These are the only keywords that make the site appear. Would anyone actually search on those keywords if they were looking for whatever the site is selling?

The major search engines like Google, have security features to prevent spamming of their listings. These security features will identify duplicate websites and they will not be listed. This means that no one searching for the website's keywords will find one of these sites. The seller has sabotaged any chance of running a successful business by selling the same website to hundreds of victims.

Some of the scammers find abandoned domain names for websites out of business and re-register that name. This gives them the appearance of being on the internet a long time through archive.org records.

Another related scam is the 'Established Web Hosting' scam. The Internet is full of failed webhosting businesses. There are also thousands of webhosting companies that range from incompetent to downright criminal. You do not want a company that has such a reputation. Anyone can start a webhosting business as a reseller with a legitimate hosting company or by setting up a Linux system on their home DSL line. A webhosting company has NO VALUE. Customers have value. When a webhosting company sells out, they sell their customers to another company, not their website and they would never sell to an individual.

You can find legitimate websites too. There are honest web designers who will put together a website and sell it. This is not much different from buying a template. These sellers will not make outrageous claims or show proof of income screenshots. Some of these people are also reselling stolen templates. They will purchase a CD of professional templates, then post one at a time on eBay claiming it is their own creation. They may also offer a cheap template and then charge a high customization fee outside of eBay to add your custom wording and company name. They may also push a specific webhosting company onto the buyer. They own the webhosting company which means they now have a high monthly payment for their low priced auction.

There are legitimate websites and legitimate established businesses on eBay, although they may not be profitable. Do your homework.

Watch for auctions that are full of contradictions and prey on those seeking their own business. No one sells an established online business for a bargain price. Look at the sellers feedback for Negatives and Mutually Withdrawn comments. Check the registration date of the domain name in whois. If the domain has only been registered a few months then how could they be an established business?

Any seller who cannot provide proof of income for the site is a scammer. Proof means quarterly reports from their accountant. What? They do not have an accountant? Then they are not running a real business. Real, money making businesses have corporate structures and legal accounting requirements. Never buy a sole-proprietorship business that you 'can run from your home'. These are all scams.

TELEPHONE SCAMS

Beware of anyone who wants your telephone number too badly. Some scammers will try to obtain your telephone number and name by pretending to be interested in an auction. They will call your number and ask for you by name which makes them sound legitimate. They will pretend to be a credit card company, a telephone company, the police, or some other entity accusing you of wrongdoing. When you protest your innocence they will need to 'verify' your information and ask for your social security number or credit card numbers, maybe your eBay or PayPal passwords if they pretend to be calling from those companies. They may only ask for the last four digits of a credit card for 'security reasons' They only need the last four digits to obtain some types of credit report access. No one will ever call you on the phone and ask for your social security number. Anyone who calls you and asks for information, no matter who they claim to be or what company they claim to be working for or what product they claim to be selling or what charity they claim to represent, is a trying to pull a scam. Even if your Caller ID shows they are who they say they are, it is fake. Scammers can setup special telephone systems or use special phone services that will display anything they want on your Caller ID. If your Caller ID shows Out Of Area, Anonymous, or Unknown, then you know the caller is fraudulent because they are hiding their caller ID information.

LOOK-ALIKE ID's

Beware of look-alike eBay ID's. A scammer can change his user ID to look like a legitimate seller's ID by simply changing the number or swapping two letters. ebayuser12345 may sell laptops and ebayuesr12345 may be a scammer who recently changed his user ID so he could send fake second chance offers to bidders of the real laptop seller's auctions or post look-alike auctions.

WANT ADS

EBay has a special section for want ads. Posting want ads in the main listings is a violation of eBay rules. EBay would be a mess if everyone started polluting the title searches with endless want ads. No one would be able to find items to buy. People who post want ads in regular listings are inconsiderate of other members of eBay and in particularly of the group they are spamming. That is right, this is simply another form of spamming.

Scammers can use want ads to draw attention to their auction and trick viewers into clicking links that lead outside of eBay or that lead to pages requesting the user's password for eBay. They may appeal to honest eBayer's who are trying to report these listings with fake 'report this listing' links which lead to look-alike eBay webpages.

If you see a want ad in the main listings, report it using the Report This Auction link at the bottom of the eBay page.

BAIT AND SWITCH AUCTIONS

You just saw a TV commercial for Product X-Amazing so you search eBay and there are ten listings for X-Amazing. You click one and see the actual item being sold is Y-Amazing which is claimed to be just as good as X-Amazing. Y-Amazing is using X-Amazing's name to draw auction viewers. They are offering one product in the title and selling a different product. This is deceptive even if the seller is clear in the auction what is being sold. They have used deceptive tactics to draw in bidders. Some sellers may offer X-Amazing and then ship Y-Amazing which is in a similar box without telling the buyer they are shipping a different product. Feedback will usually reveal such scammers from previous customer complaints. Don't trust bait and switch sellers.

Some sellers use well known designer clothing brand names in the title, then show photos of that brand, but in the small print they are actually selling a look-alike or knock-off product. They depend on buyers to make a quick decision and not read the auction closely.

Listing a popular brand name to spam searches and attract viewers only to offer a different product than the one listed in the title is bait and switch. This is a violation of eBay rules too. Sellers that resort to this type of tactic cannot be trusted.

ONE CENT EBOOKS

One Cent eBooks are actually a long sales pitch. They usually claim you can make a lot of money following their advice. The book then recommends a website where you have to pay a membership or monthly fee or where the website owner has a list of companies where they will receive an affiliate bonus for sales made from their site. These eBooks are also used for illegal schemes such as pyrmaid or multi level marketing schemes. The scammer may openly offer to pay you a percentage for every victim you bring to his site and for every person the victim in-turn brings in(that is a pyramid scheme), you receive a percentage. This is completely illegal. Some of the eBooks actually recommend committing fraud and give the procedure to do it.

I saw a TV commercial for a product that claimed to repair eyeglass scratches. It is a solution that fills in the scratches in polymer eyeglasses. I wanted to try it out to see if it could fix Plexiglas scratches easily so I checked eBay first. EBay is a great place to find infomercial bargains. The people who bought the infomercial item last month are often selling it this month at a discount. Many infomercial companies add unauthorized charges to your final price. I prefer to buy things like this through eBay where I can control the payments with PayPal. I found a listing for this product, let's call it PRODUCT-X but when I started reading the description more closely, I realized it was another product with a similar name and similar design. That should have been my first tip-off. They even had 'As Seen On TV' in the auction listing. I doubt this product was on TV unless it was a Dateline story. The claims were the same and I thought it could be the same base product. It is not uncommon for several companies to sell the same generic chemicals under different names. The price was 0.99 opening bid and $14.95 shipping. That should have been my second tip off about this seller. Low opening bid with no one competing or bidding the product up while the seller still had multiple listings. Lowball price and high shipping. The seller still had decent feedback. Only two negatives in the past month and over 300 positives in the same time. I put in a bid on one of twenty auctions that were about to close and won for 0.99 plus $14.95 shipping. I sent PayPal payment. The seller waited a full week before shipping and then shipped by first class mail. The auction description deceptively listed 'Flat Rate Shipping' and did not specify first class. That should have been my third tip-off. When the product arrived, I tried it and it did not work. I had plenty of warning signs, but I ignored them. I had so many positive experiences, I dropped my guard. This seller used deceptive keywords to bait and switch customers, this seller had excessive shipping costs, and they failed to list their shipping method in the auction. It was only $15 out of my pocket, but it was a lesson to pay attention to the warning signs. Never trust a bait-and-switch seller.

By the way, I should have Googled the original company first and I would have found that the product did not work.

Sell a Link Scam

Many information scams are actually 'sell-a-link' scams. These are commonly titled "Make Money on News Events" or "EBay Secrets no one knows but me" or "Cash in on Russia" or "Work At Home Businesses". The seller offers an auction for anywhere from 99 cents to 99 dollars. The winning bidder is sent a link to a website. The seller owns website or receives some commission for sending people to it. The website could be a scam. That may be why the information was only 99 cents, the seller expects to scam the buyer for much more later. Sometimes sellers offer a special password and login for these sites to make them sound special. The login page may be completely fake and anyone can access the website. These are always scams. Some sellers email a webpage of links to sites with Work-At-Home information or other information that anyone could find with a simple Google search.

No honest seller can auction a link to a website or a list of links to other websites. These auctions are never legitimate.

Selling a link to a website is a scam.

These include Wholesale distributor lists, How To Get a Free iPod information, Drop-Shipper lists and similar information offerings.

There are dishonest sellers who run auctions that appear to be selling an item, but in fact they are selling a list or other information. These sellers may say in their title "New Plasma TV", but in the small print of the auction they are offering a list of wholesale suppliers of TV's. This list is useless and you can find better deals on the Internet. The title may say **Authentic Top Designer Purse Handbag New Wholesale List** and show a prominent picture of a designer handbag for a 99 cent Buy-It-Now price. Remember, if it sounds too good to be true, it is. These auctions are designed to trick impulsive buyers into buying now without reading the entire auction listing. The auction is not selling a handbag, they are selling a worthless list of wholesalers.

Some sellers offer one cent lists to draw in victims for later scams. Others sell lists for $20 and try to make their auctions look like they are selling the actual item.
These lists promote the seller's business and attempt to trick buyers into thinking they are receiving a special price. These may also be connected to illegal pyramid schemes where the sellers want to generate members or sales so they will receive a percentage. They can also link to fake websites used to collect credit card numbers that have no products to ship. These lists often recommend fraudulent drop shipping companies or fraudulent wholesalers.

These sellers depend on inexperienced buyers acting rashly and then being unwilling to leave negative feedback for such a small purchase. These sellers are showing an item, offering a low price, but sending a list or ebook instead of the pictured item. Information auctions are a type of bait and switch scam.

Many of the auctions offering information on how to obtain a free plasma TV or free iPod are actually e-books advising buyers how to commit fraud. Following the information in them could result in jail time for the buyer. One of the most common among these scams is how to defraud gambling sites where the seller advises the buyer to use the stolen funds to purchase the item desired.

BRAND NEW PROFESSIONAL HD VIDEO CAMERA wholesale list

BRAND NEW HD VIDEO CAMERA WHOLESALE LIST

ADD ME TO YOUR FAVORITES SELLER LIST

CHECK OUT OUR STORE FOR MORE BARGAINS

This auction appears to offer an HD Camera at a wholesale-list price. It is actually for a worthless list of wholesale dealers. The list promotes the company that posted this auction by listing various websites they created as the top sites to visit. Their negative feedback shows they have scammed many customers.

CHOICE AUCTIONS

This is not so much a scam as questionable seller ethics. I don't know exactly why, but sellers who use Choice Auctions are frequently shady or incompetent. For one thing, these auctions are a violation of eBay policy. If the eBay police see this auction or it is reported to them, it will be pulled. Here is how it works. A seller offers an item like a Movie DVD and the winner has his choice of any of three titles available. This seems simple, but the bidders are not all bidding on the same item. It is not an auction for a specific item.

The seller must pick one item and sell it or list three auctions. This may seem silly, but by offering a choice, the bidders are not competing for the same item. This is not fair to bidders and that is why eBay does not allow choice auctions. The example does not seem not so shady, but the movie seller is a shady character and it turned out he was selling pirate copies. Anyone offering such auctions should be avoided. They may actually be selling pirate copies of movies, or they may not ship anything at all. Choice auctions are favored by shady characters. EBay will catch up to them soon enough.

> *I once purchased a plant pedestal on eBay and the seller offered a 'choice' of finishes. I did not think about this as a choice auction, but that is exactly what it was. It was not clear from the auction that this choice cost extra. I bid on the item and when I won, I paid the bid amount and told them what finish I wanted. I PayPal'd payment and waited until the item should have arrived, but no item showed up. I emailed and the seller said I had not selected my finish. I replied and quoted my original order which did specify the finish. Then they told me I had to pay extra for a finish. This was in the small print of the auction, but it was not clear due to their poor English. I paid the extra $14 and again specified the finish because I wanted the stand. Then the seller again emailed asking what finish I wanted. I had already told them at least three times. Weeks later I finally received the pedestal. The seller was very difficult to deal with and extremely slow to ship or respond. This is a good example of what you run into when dealing with choice auctions. I avoid choice auctions now.*

ELLIPSES ...

Never trust a buyer or seller who uses excessive ellipses in emails, auctions, or if he uses ellipses in place of commas.

> *I use this address because the ebay email address is not working....i have the laptop now also...if you are interested...make me an offer ....then we can discuss about it. Thank you lots.*

This is clearly an email from a scammer. It uses ellipses instead of periods and the grammar is terrible. This was a real email from a real scammer and he was lying about the Ebay message center not working.

I'm New, No PayPal

Beware of sellers who claim to be new and use excuses for not having a PayPal account or for not being able to use their PayPal account.

"I've reached my maximum limit" or *"I am a new user and don't have an account"* or users who refer to nopaypal.com as the reason they do not have a paypal account. These are all common tactics of scammers who want to receive payments by Western Union or other means. They can setup a new account with no feedback and justify not offering PayPal with these claims.

It only takes a few minutes to setup a PayPal account so there is no reason for someone to not have an account. Anyone who has reached their limit for a personal account can click a button to upgrade to a Premiere account and accept more payments. Besides, personal accounts cannot be used for auctions anyway so this person is not supposed to be using their personal PayPal account for auctions.

Beware of any seller who claims they do not use PayPal because they do not want to pay the fees. This is a common line used by scammers. Beware of anyone who makes excuses explaining why they cannot accept PayPal payments. Their PayPal account may have been disabled because of fraud.

Catalog Auctions

This does not mean buying a catalog that is itself antique or collectable. A seller offering to sell his company's catalog of items he wants to sell to you sell is violating eBay rules. The seller is not selling an actual item, he is selling an advertising tool. Basically, he is using eBay to advertise which is against eBay rules. You can buy and sell the 1976 Sears and Roebuck catalog, but not your own catalog. Sell the items from it instead. If they are any good, people will buy them.

Many catalog sellers claim their catalogs have super bargains or wholesale prices. They may add coupons worth hundreds of dollars. To redeem these coupons, you must purchase from the seller's website and you may find their prices are not the wholesale bargains that were promised. They may also charge excessive shipping.

Would you trust giving your credit card number to a seller who has already violated eBay rules and deceived you by claiming his catalog offered discounts that were in fact inflated prices which were then discounted?

These sellers frequently do not admit the catalogs they are selling are their catalog and may give an elaborate story about how they found the company and how they want to share their find with others.

Report *'buy my catalog'* auctions to eBay.

User ID Change

When an eBay user changes their ID, a new icon appears by it for 30 days. EBay users do not normally change their name frequently. If you are looking at an expensive item and the user has changed their ID, take a look at past sales and at their past ID history which is linked on the feedback page. What does it show? Did the seller previously sell postcards and now they are suddenly selling cars and expensive jewelry? Something is wrong here. Did the user ID change from ebaybob101 to ebay-car-emporium? It looks strange to change from a personal ID to a specific business type ID. Something is fishy here.

Payment to Third Party

Make sure that you pay the actual seller. The seller's name should be in the eBay confirmation email. If their account has been hijacked this could be changed, but scammers often do not bother to change the name or phone number. If the seller's name is Bob and you are asked to send payment to Raj, there is something fishy about the transaction. If you check the user ID history and see that it was changed ten days ago from ebay-bob to ebaylaptopscammer123 that is one warning sign, and if they ask for payments to be sent to Raj then that is a second sign. Why was the old user ID for Bob but the seller claims their name is now Raj? This is clearly a compromised account.

Fake Phone Numbers

Don't trust a seller just because he claims to be in the USA and has a USA phone number. You can Google for "area code XXX" where XXX is the area code of the phone number to find out where the number is located. This area code check does not always work. Scammers can setup VOIP(voice over IP) telephone service using stolen credit cards. This allows them to setup a phone number that appears to be in one state of the US, when the scammer may be answering the phone in another country. This is common in auto fraud where they want to appear as if they are in the USA. The person who answers the phone will usually have a heavy accent.

Email Addresses Confusion

If a seller lists one email address in an auction and then contacts you from a different address saying they are having problems with their other email address, this is a sure sign you are dealing with a scammer. This always means the other fraudulent email address was disabled and the scammer had to find a new one to use. Never do business with anyone who changes their email address like this, especially if they are using free email services(like hotmail.com, yahoo.com, gmail.com, etc).

Never trust a seller who claims to be in one country, but uses an email address from another country. If they claim to be in Canada but mail from a yahoo.com.uk address, they are a scammer.

No Longer Registered

Look for excessive numbers of '**no longer registered user**' notations in a seller's feedback profile. Criminals with time and resources will setup a hundred or more accounts and swap feedback among them to build fake feedback histories. As these accounts are identified by eBay and disabled, it becomes clear in the feedback profiles of the remaining accounts. They have many no longer registered messages for accounts that were all created within a short time period of each other.

Out of the Country

Never believe any eBay seller who is selling something and claims they are out of the country on a business trip. This is always a scam. No one sells on eBay while they are out of the country. Legitimate sellers will wait until they return. No one *suddenly* moves out of the country and needs to sell items still in the USA. They will have taken care of things like selling excess items before moving or they will give them to a relative who will take care of the sale. The relative is the seller then.

Scammers often use this lie to trick buyers into sending payments outside of the USA.

USD Scams

Any auction that shows its location in the USA and then uses the abbreviation USD is a scam. USD stands for US Dollars and is used to differentiate US Dollars from Canadian, Australian and other countries using a currency called Dollars.

No one in the USA ever uses USD as a currency identifier. Use of USD is common in foreign countries. Many foreign scammers will pretend to be US citizens who have moved overseas, are out of the country on business, or who are in the military.

I am offering this new car for only $12,000.00 USD I took a job here in the country of Nigeria for the OIL MINISTRY and need to seal it most quickly. The car is in New Jersey and i will ship for free if you can pay today.

I will sell this laptop to you now for $800 USD and free shipping. I am from New Jersey and I am going to school as a student here in Nigeria so I need the money most quickly.

These are obvious scams. No one goes to Nigeria to attend school.

Anyone using commas for decimals who claims to be in the USA or claims to be American is likely a scammer. Non English speaking countries often use commas for decimals. English speaking countries use periods for decimals.

Comma for decimal example(this person is clearly not in the US Army)

I am offering this new car for only $12 000,00 I am in the US Army and had to be stationed over seas here. I must sell it quickly as possible please Western Union payment fast.

If they use USD or commas for decimals, or cannot speak English well, it should be clear they are not from the USA.

Another common scam is claiming an item is in the USA but the currency of the auction is for another country. You may see auctions with the location listed as the UK but instead of the currency being in GBP, it is in German Marks or in Australia dollars AU. The currency should match the country the item is located in or be in US Dollars. US Dollars are used in many countries as well as local currency.

Haunted, Cursed, Blessed, Psychic Scams

These scammers purchase cheap items, tack a good story onto them, and sell them at a huge profit.

The crucifix blessed by the pope? It has never been in Europe. The gothic wood carving statue blessed, or cursed, by some coven of witches no one every heard of...what are you paying for? Nothing. Anyone can claim an item is blessed, cursed, or haunted because they do not have to prove anything. A certificate of authenticity also means nothing. This is a scam targeted at the gullible.

Tarot card reading, Psychic reading by email. Your fortune by email. I can tell your fortune right now *"If you paid for one of these, you just got scammed"*. So far, I have not been wrong.

There are two types of tarot or fortune readers. One gives a really bad reading so you never return and the other gives a pending warning or some other nonsense that is meant to cause fear. This leads you to want another reading from this person at a higher price. There are many self proclaimed psychics offering readings. You can be certain the first reading will require an important second reading for a higher price otherwise catastrophe could befall you.

Are you paying a basement price for a star chart, a spiritual guide? The seller usually has ten or so pre-made charts and they randomly pick one to send to every buyer. Tarot cards are just as easy. Look in the instructions that come with the cards and make up ten readings. Make sure that every new customer starts on the first reading and receives a new reading with every subsequent purchase.

Slow, Late Payments

Scammers almost never pay immediately after the auction closes. If a scammer buyer wins one of your auctions and takes more than ten days to send payment, it usually means the payment is either counterfeit, or if it is a check, it will bounce. They may also report a money order as lost or stolen before you can cash it. Hold shipments until the payment has cleared for anyone who pays late.

You can also check the buyers recent buying history. Use the advanced search to check a buyers past buying history. Have they recently purchased several cars? Several expensive pieces of electronics? That is not normal for anyone.

I saw your interest..

Beware of anyone who contacts you because they saw your bid on another auction. Since eBay started hiding bidder id's this is not as much of a problem. They may obtain your email elsewhere though and make the same offer. Scammers routinely look at high priced auctions and try to convince bidders they have the same item at a better price. EBay has started hiding bidder identities on high value items. Scammers may still contact early bidders or bidders on lower price auctions.

Anyone who contacts you through eBay to sell you anything outside of eBay is a scammer.

For A Friend

I listed this for a friend, contact them with questions, I dont know anything about it, so direct all questions to my friend at notascammer@somescammersite.com.

Why did their friend not list the item themselves? Why does the seller feel it is so important to make it clear they are not the person selling the item when it is their account the item is listed under? If the seller is selling the item, then the seller is selling the item. Not their friend. This is a common scheme to avoid responsibility for the outcome of the auction. The seller can claim they had nothing to do with the damaged or misrepresented item because they were selling it for someone else. There frequently is no 'friend'.

This is a common tactic to force bidders to contact the person outside of eBay. By forcing anyone with questions to contact the other party without using the Message Center, the seller can offer to make a direct sale to everyone who responds. Contact the seller through the Message Center with a simple question. If the seller does not respond or insists you contact them through the listed email address, then you know the auction was a scam.

I have found that most of the time the seller will never respond to questions through the Message Center which indicates they are afraid to communicate in a way that can be monitored by eBay.

You are not buying from their friend, you are not bidding on their friend's auction. You are buying from the seller and bidding on their auction. They should answer questions and take responsibility for their auction.

Excessive Shipping

Never trust a seller who has excessive shipping costs. It is acceptable, even necessary for a seller to charge more than actual shipping costs. It is not appropriate to charge excessive amounts. Common sense will usually reveal anyone charging excessive shipping. A small digital camera that costs $4.99 Buy-It-Now with $40 shipping is clearly excessive. A camera for $30 and $12.95 shipping is more in line with what an honest seller might charge.

Excessive Shipping can be reported, but there are certain requirements. A seller offering a CD with 'flat rate shipping' of $20 and an opening bid of $0.99 is not necessarily violating eBay's rules. If this were a Buy-It-Now auction, the seller would be in violation. If the seller said shipping was by Priority Mail or first class mail, they would be in violation because those services cost much less than the quoted fee for the size/weight of the CD.

Excessive shipping is sometimes used by dishonest sellers who expect returns. They will accept the return to resell, but do not refund the shipping. This is common in designer clothing, computer parts, and electronics.

Cancelled Bids

Beware sellers who cancel your bid and then contact you for ANY reason. A legitimate seller will never cancel your bid and then contact you. If they want information or want to sell direct, it's a scam.

ONE CENT AUCTIONS

Beware of one cent auctions. These are either feedback scams designed to inflate the sellers feedback so they can commit larger fraud or they are scams to obtain personal information or to sell you something that will cost more later. Scammers sometimes use low price auctions to attract bids from inexperienced members who make easy targets for bigger scams.

Legitimate sellers can start an auction at one cent or one dollar, but if they have several such auctions and there is no bidding activity, something is wrong. They would not keep listing the auctions and losing money on every one. It is legitimate to start an auction at one cent, not to end an auction at one cent.

When a seller uses a very low price as a starting price and lists many auctions for the same item which are either not closing or closing with single bids, that indicates a scam.

The seller may have a low price and high shipping to circumvent eBay listing fees. EBay has cracked down on excessive shipping auctions, but some fall through the cracks. A one cent auction offering an e-Book by download with $5 shipping is a scam because the e-Book is available as a downloaded. Sellers cannot charge shipping or handling fees on downloaded items on eBay so this seller is side stepping that rule.

Auctions with Buy-It-Now options at these price levels are easily identified as scams. No seller pays $0.50 to post an auction listing so they can sell an item for $0.01 or $0.99 especially if there is no shipping or free shipping. It is not worth the time to list and the seller is not making money. Selling items for under $5 makes no sense.

Scammers use low priced auctions to trick people into subscribing to useless services or into paying for other get-rich-quick schemes. They may offer an ebook that instructs the buyer to join a $29.95 per month website. Suddenly this auction involves more than one cent.

Scammers use low priced auctions to run up their feedback making them appear to be a legitimate trusted seller.

Low priced auctions that cost more to list than the seller makes are guarantees of some type of scam.

EXCUSES

Beware of any seller who gives excuses about why you cannot inspect an expensive item that is in your state or gives excuses about why they cannot provide additional photos of a car or motorcycle or other expensive item they are selling. You can always ask for a photograph of the odometer or door sticker plate on a vehicle. If the seller cannot provide it, they do not have the vehicle.

NOT REALLY SELLING

"We are not actually selling iPod" Any auction that appears to offer an iPod, but then claims they are not actually selling an iPod(or any other item) is usually a scam. These may be information scams, or pyramid scheme scams. If the seller has to state they are not selling what they appear to be selling, something is wrong.

COMPLETELY GUARANTEED

Honest sellers often offer satisfaction guarantees. Don't be lulled into trusting a seller just because they do offer a guarantee. Be especially wary if their guarantee sounds too good to be true.

A scammer can guarantee anything. They are usually using stolen accounts so they will never have to honor any guarantee anyway. Free shipping, no problem, guaranteed return with 100% of your money back and your original shipping, no problem. Whatever it takes to con someone out of their money. The scammer never has to honor any guarantee. Beware of any guarantee that sounds too good to be true. Honest sellers do offer guarantees, but they also have expenses and will not state a guarantee in such a way that they seem to say *'go ahead and take advantage of me'*. The *'take advantage of me'* type phrases are how scammers attract victims.

MISCATEGORIZED ITEMS

Scammers often intentionally miscategorize items. They will post items to unrelated categories where they have no competition for the item. They may post an expensive Samurai sword to a video game related group.

Beware of vehicles posted in the Parts category of eBay Motors. Scammers often do this to attract buyers who are searching by keyword and do not notice the category. Scammers list in this area to avoid scrutiny of those who watch the auto groups for scams.

ASK TRICK QUESTIONS

Scammers often offer vehicles in the eBay Motors area. If you see an auction and you are unsure about the seller, ask a trick question.
You may be looking for a classic Volkswagon Beetle from the 60's, Ask the seller if the radiator leaks. There is no radiator in this car. If the seller says it is new with no leaks, you know they are a scammer. They do not even have the car and know nothing about it.

Compare the description, does the seller show a V6 in the photo but claim it is a V8 engine in the description? Talk to the seller by phone before paying for any expensive item, especially a vehicle.

DUPLICATE AUCTIONS

Scammers are often lazy. They will re-use the same scam auction over and over. If you see a suspect auction, copy and paste the title into the advanced search box and click the option to search closed auctions. Look for the same item in past auctions under other accounts, especially if those accounts are now disabled. If you see the exact same auction listed under other accounts, this is the same scammer posting the same auction with a new hijacked account.

You can also search the description for unique groups of words.

Urgency

Beware of any auction that has a sense of urgency. Scammers want to cause panic in the buyer so they will send payment fast without thinking. The scammers want buyers to feel they will lose a great opportunity if they do not act hastily. Any auction that claims the seller must sell an item fast means the seller must sell the item before the police catch them.

> *I must sell this jewelry quickly to pay for emergency surgery for my little niece who was in a car accident. Contact me quickly because I must have the money by noon or they are going to cut off her life support.*

> *I am advertising locally so may cancel the auction if you do not use Buy-It-Now right away.*

Beware of anyone claiming an emergency due to surgery, divorce, accident, family death, etc. These are common scams.

Leave Me Feedback

Never leave feedback first if the other member threatens you with negative feedback. This was more important when eBay allowed sellers to leave negative feedback. I still include this advice in case eBay rules are changed in the future.

I had a buyer who actually sent this to me:

> *If you don't leave positive feedback for me, I will leave you negative feedback and report you to eBay.*

He had no reason to leave negative feedback because he received his purchase exactly as listed in the auction and he never complained or asked any follow-up questions.

Once you have left feedback, the other party is free to leave you negative feedback without worry of receiving negative feedback. If a scammer seller threatens to leave you negative feedback if you do not leave them positive feedback, DO NOT DO IT! Report them to eBay.

The person who sent the above message later admitted they intended to leave negative feedback. They never asked about a return or said what problem they had. Their real interest was in the thrill of leaving negative feedback.

Payment Agents

Beware of any seller who wants to handle payment through a Payment Agent. There is no such thing. Dishonest sellers may ask the buyer to send a Western Union payment to a Payment Agent. They may even point the buyer to an official looking website. This is a scam. Once the Western Union payment is sent, the buyer will never hear from the seller again. Beware of any seller who wants to use an unusual payment method like this.

Escrow services act as an intermediary to the transaction. The buyer does not pay the seller directly; instead they send payment to an Escrow company. When the buyer receives the goods and approves of them, they notify the Escrow Company, which then releases the funds to the seller minus their commission. The only escrow company eBay recommends is escrow.com. Escrow is generally only used for very expensive items like cars. There are a number of escrow frauds out there. Some dishonest sellers setup fake Escrow websites. Once the fake Escrow Company receives payment, the buyer never receives anything. This is why eBay only recommends escrow.com and warns members to be wary of other companies. Any escrow company that uses the name PayPal, eBay or Square Trade as part of their name is fraudulent.

No legitimate escrow service would ever accept a Western Union payment, or ask anyone for their bank information, or to use an e-anything type payment service. No legitimate escrow service will ever ask for a payment to be made to any person or to a business other than their business name which should be their URL. Beware of any seller who wants to use a different escrow service from escrow.com.

Here is how the escrow scam works. The scammer sets up a website that appears to be an escrow company. They then sell an expensive vehicle on eBay and refer the buyer to their fake escrow company claiming they have used the company many times and had good experiences with them. The buyer sends payment to what they think is a third party escrow company and then they never hear from the seller or the escrow company again. Or a seller may ship the goods and never hear from the buyer or escrow company again.

Fake escrow sites are one of the biggest frauds on eBay because they can obtain the most money. If a buyer or seller wants to use a specific escrow service, other than escrow.com, for an expensive purchase, BEWARE!

You can check out an escrow service by looking at the whois information for their website. If the site was registered recently, it is obvious they are not legitimate. Beware of any escrow company that has not existed at least three years. If it is registered anywhere other than the USA, it is a scam. If the domain name or website claims affiliation with a major corporation like eBay, Western Union, or PayPal, you know it is a scam. Pretty much, it is safe to assume they are all scams if they are not escrow.com.

Escrow services should be listed on the state's corporate website. Every state has a website where corporate information can be searched to find the corporation(or LLC) name, address, and how long they have been in business for any corporation in that state.

From the other side, a seller sells a vehicle or expensive item and the buyer insists on a certain escrow company for their protection. The seller agrees. The escrow company sends the seller a notice saying the payment has been received and the seller should release the goods. Only when the goods have been sent or received will the funds be released to the seller. The seller either allows pick-up or ships the vehicle and never hears from the buyer or escrow company again. The escrow site was a fake setup by the scam buyer. There never was a payment. It was a trick to make the seller release the vehicle or other expensive item.

PayPal Escrow is the same as a regular escrow scam. The scammer tries to trick the buyer or seller into thinking PayPal has an escrow program. They do NOT. Do not send the item, you will never see your money. Anyone who wants to use PayPal Escrow is a scammer. There is no such program.

The only approved escrow company for eBay purchases is escrow.com. No other escrow company should be used.

CERTIFICATES OF AUTHENTICITY

Some items require a certificate of authenticity to be sold on eBay such as celebrity signatures. Some collectible scenes have well established certification authorities, but some do not. If you see an item offered with a certificate of authenticity, make sure the certificate is valid. Anyone can print a nice looking certificate using an inkjet printer. If you are paying for an item that is supposed to be authentic, make sure it is. The seller should offer the option to return the item for a refund if you are not satisfied or do not feel the item is authentic. Beware of any seller offering an authentic item with a Certificate of Authenticity who will not take returns.

SECOND CHANCE OFFER FRAUD

When an auction closes and the seller has more of the same item to sell, or the high bidder backs out, the seller can issue a Second Chance Offer to the other bidders. Scammers sometimes send fake second chance offers to high bidders offering them the item at their high bid. This is not the seller sending the offer, but a criminal impersonating the seller. Make sure you only respond to legitimate second chance offers.

Fake Second Chance offers can appear in your Messages Center. Some scammers will use the eBay message center to send a message to another member and will make it look like a second chance offer. Real second chance offers will appear as eBay system messages which are different from regular user messages. Real Second Chance offers will say "eBay Second Chance Offer for Item..." in the subject. Messages from other members will say "Message from eBay Member".

When someone is selling a rare one-of-a-kind antique, a second chance offer is pretty fishy because they would not have two identical items, but when selling a game console or electronics it is not uncommon to make a second chance offer. Make sure the offer is from the actual seller and through eBay by checking your My Messages console

Never accept a second chance offer that is emailed outside of eBay. You have no way of determining who sent such an offer. EBay has begun hiding bidder names on auctions with high values to reduce this type of fraud.

FREE VEHICLE SHIPPING

Free shipping is a common method to attract bidders. Free shipping on large items is not common. A seller who offers to ship a used car that is being sold below book value for free is a scammer. A seller offering an expensive flat panel TV for a fraction of its value is likely a scammer and if he offers free shipping he is a scammer. They can promise anything because they never have to deliver. Beware of anyone offering free shipping on large and expensive items, especially vehicles.

"Beware of this Scam" Scam

Beware of any auction(or any website) that gives a warning about a scam and then tries to sell you the 'real thing'. This is a common technique scammers use to build confidence and trust. They will appear to help auction viewers by warning them about others on eBay selling counterfeit or otherwise bad items, but their items is great and wonderful so you should buy it. Some of these scammers actually slam their own product, but the buyer does not know it is the same product.

> *Beware of others selling fake Chinese made knock-offs. You can spot these scammers by the orange boxes they come in and the poor quality of the seams and connectors. Our product was produced in Hong Kong and is guaranteed original.*

These types of statements usually indicate a scam.

Click HERE

You are browsing your favorite category and in the gallery image you see an explicit image of a naked woman. This is unusual since you are in the Lawn Tractor Parts area. You click on the auction and there is an explicit image with a message below it 'click to enlarge' When you click the image a page pops up asking your eBay password to continue. This is a fake website setup by the scammer.

Beware of auctions with lots of Click Here links.

"Click Here To Watch This Auction"
"Click Here to Add Me To Your Favorites"
"Click HERE to see other auctions"
"Click HERE to see my PayPal History"
"Click Here To Pay by PayPal, don't use the checkout button"

These links often lead to look-alike pages that request your eBay or PayPal password.

Beware of auctions containing PayPal links that request your PayPal password. If you click on a link in the description area of an auction that goes to a page requesting that you login to PayPal or eBay, STOP! This is a common tactic of phishers. They hijack an account and then post a fake auction with links to look-alike websites that are designed to look like eBay or PayPal. They may offer Dutch Auctions for many low priced items and ask people to click a PayPal button in the auction to pay. A Dutch auction allows them to scam many people with one auction listing. This button goes to a fake look-alike PayPal website. Never use PayPal links inside an auction or eBay links that request your user ID or any other personal information. Always check for the https and verify the url.

Never use a checkout button that is in the listing. These lead to fraudulent payment sites that collect personal information and credit card numbers.

Only use the eBay checkout button in your MyEbay page or at the top of the auction in the official information area.

A variation on this scam occurs when the scammer uses HTML code or a large transparent GIF image in the auction. This creates a full page invisible link. When the auction viewer clicks anywhere in the auction, they are redirected to a look-alike eBay login page which was setup by the scammer. Once the scammer has obtained the person's eBay user ID and password, they may transfer back to the auction or they may transfer to a 'buy now' fake page with an even better price as long as the person pays by clicking the PayPal link. The PayPal link also goes to the scammer's site so they can steal the visitors PayPal password.

Install the MyLittleMole.com toolbar to catch these scam sites before you enter your information.

DROP SHIP SCAMS

You may see auctions offering information on drop shippers or receive spam regarding these companies. Drop shippers are companies that sell items to you at a wholesale price and will ship directly to your customer. You sell item X on eBay, then you login to your drop shipper's website and tell them to ship product X to the customer and bill you the wholesale amount. Your profit is the difference between the amount you sold the item for and the amount the drop shipper charges. At least that is how drop shippers are supposed to work.

The majority of drop shipping services are scams. Commonly you will pay $100 or more or pay a monthly fee to become a member. You cannot see what they offer or pricing until after you are a member. When you do login to their database, you find their items are junk, are overpriced, or are all listed as out of stock.

Legitimate drop shipping companies will never sell items at a large discount to individual sellers. Unless you sign a contract guaranteeing to buy a $100,000 minimum every month, you will never receive preferred pricing and their *wholesale* prices will be higher than retail.

There are outright crooked drop shippers. These companies will charge up-front fees then when you try to order anything, the status will change to unavailable even if it was available ten seconds earlier. If you just sold this item on eBay, you have a customer expecting an item to be shipped and you have a drop shipper saying the item that was available is no longer available. This creates a serious problem for the seller.

Some of these dishonest companies have nothing but junk. They purchase items from China for $0.25 and then try to sell them to you for $7 while telling you the retail price is $30. If you check eBay first, you will see that no one is buying the items that are already listed, and they are listed for much less, maybe even less than $7. No one wants a flower vase from China and no one in their right mind will pay $30 for one on eBay. These companies offer worthless products. If the products were good, they would be selling the products themselves.

Some of these dishonest drop shipping companies hire people in India to go around to message boards posting praise for their company and giving false testimonials. They also setup fake drop shipper rating websites where their site or their clone sites are the only ones recommended.

Some of the drop shippers are not drop shippers, but are acting as middlemen, or agents. They are not the actual drop shipper, they are fronting for a drop shipper. Don't fall for the eBay drop shipper scam. If there were a good drop shipper, everyone would know.

"Please send to my sister at this address which is not mine, this is a gift...please don't speak about ebay, the item number or cost when you ship the item as it is a gift, oh also please use my below address as the return address..and wrapped up with a tape wrap carefully. If you can not to do this refund my paypal payment and I will find another seller who will help me. Thanks."

This should be a clear scam from the detailed instructions, the request to ship to someone else other than the buyer, the request to falsify the return address and especially the mention of cancellation. The scammer closes by almost threatening the seller if they do not comply.

The terms of the sale were set in the auction. The buyer does not set the terms of the sale, the seller and eBay do. The buyer has no right, legal or otherwise, to make any of these demands on the seller and cannot demand a refund if the seller is unwilling to follow their instructions.

If the seller does follow these instructions, the buyer can file for a refund through PayPal because the shipment was not sent to the buyer's address. The destination address may not even exist so the buyer expects the package to be returned to him, which is why he wants his address as the return address.

Make sure you have a tracking number and only ship to the Confirmed PayPal address. If you are suspicious, DO NOT SHIP. If the buyer is actually giving it as a gift, they can reship it themselves. Their gift is not the sellers responsibility.

The odds are, this is an scam!

"Can you ship to my friend, it is their birthday, it has to be there on time, you won't let me down will you"

Translate *"Ship to my friend"* to mean *"I'm using a stolen credit card or hijacked PayPal account"* and this scam becomes clear. The buyer contacts the seller and says they are about to send payment, but they request that the item be shipped to their friend or family member in Nigeria or some other country. They will then pay through PayPal using a stolen credit card. When PayPal receives the chargeback, they reverse the payment in the seller's PayPal account.

Hello Seller,

It's pleased me to winning your auction, how are you today? hope all is good, I will be paying you via my paypal account, send me your paypal email address, item cost and the shipping cost to my wife address below in Nigeria. She is a student there.

Do get back to me today so i can make the payment once. And have a good day.

Best Regards,
Nigerian Scammer

Never trust anyone who requests a purchase be shipped to their friend in Russia, Nigeria, Romania, the Philippines, or Indonesia or any address other than the one listed as the credit card billing address or the PayPal account Confirmed address. Only ship to the verified PayPal address of the buyer. Send-to-a-friend usually means the buyer is using a stolen credit card and needs the item shipped to a different name than the one on the victim's credit card.

> *Foreign scammers setup fraud centers in the USA. They will use a hotel room or rent an apartment using fake identification. They hire drug addicts and immigrants to pickup Western Union or Money Order payments for them. They only sell to out of state buyers to avoid local law enforcement. The criminals then wire the money to Romania, Nigeria or other countries. If they think the police may be closing in, they jump on an airplane and go home.*

Beware of any seller who offers an expensive item below cost and then is willing to accept a 60% down payment. Scammers frequently offer expensive items such as vehicles and then request a down payment, holding fee, or some other up-front fee. The scammers are not concerned with collecting the $10,000 for a vehicle they are offering. They want to collect the $2,000 down payment from as many people as possible.

PayPal eCheck Fraud

A scammer wins one of your auctions. They send payment through PayPal by selecting an eCheck which should transfer the money from their checking account. The scammer makes sure they do not have enough funds in their checking account for the payment to clear. Then the eCheck bounces and the clearing date changes to two weeks when PayPal will automatically try again. The seller does not know this has occurred, only the buyer. The scammer then complains about not receiving the item and claims the eCheck did clear but PayPal has made an error or the seller is not reading their account correctly. The scammer has the bank statement that they will gladly send as proof. Of course, it is a Photoshoped version and can say anything they want it to say. The buyer may file an Item Not Received dispute with eBay or threaten negative feedback to force the seller to ship early.

Never ship to a buyer until the payment has cleared and you see the funds available in your Paypal account. Beware of any buyer who tries to pressure you to ship early. If an eCheck has not cleared in 4 days, it will probably never clear.

I have found that 99% of eChecks I receive clear with no problem. Your level of fraud will depend on the products you sell and who your customers are.

Don't Bid On This Item

Any auction that instructs the bidder to Not bid, is a scam. Take the sellers advice and DO NOT BID! The seller may insist interested parties contact him by email or direct viewers to a scam website in order to sell outside of eBay. It can also be a sales ploy to generate curiosity so they read the auction. An auction is an auction, and any seller who does not want you to bid on their auction is trying to pull some type of scam.

Pre-Sale Items

Some sellers offer hot items before they are actually available for sale. This may be a new hot toy before Christmas or a new gaming console. These are called Pre-Sale items. They are not called Pre-Sell items, that is incorrect. The seller is offering an item for sale that he does not have in his possession. I avoid pre-sale auctions. These auctions often sell items at prices much higher than their actual value. The same seller checks apply here that apply to regular auctions. If a seller is new and offering pre-sale items, they may not be legitimate. Pre-sale items are a good excuse to collect money early and never ship anything. Customers are not expecting to receive anything for up to 30 days. This gives a dishonest seller plenty of time to collect money before disappearing. I have found that you can purchase these items for less after they are released. Sometimes for much less only days later.

> *I was interested in starting a new website offering computer parts and video games. One particular video game I was interested in reselling stated on their website that they were available through ... we will call the company Intelegram Micros(not the real company name). I paid $100 to *this company*, one of the largest drop shipper's out there, I filled out the forms and was finally approved. I received my login information and logged into their website for the first time ever. The video game I was interested in reselling was out of stock with no expectation for new stock. So much for that idea. I then decided to make the best of it and offer computer parts. I looked up a specific model of computer harddrive and it cost $120 wholesale to me plus shipping. I checked Google and found hundreds of websites selling the exact same model for $80 street price. Several other items had the same result. I logged out of my account and have never logged in again. How was I supposed to buy computer parts for $120 wholesale then sell them at $80 and make a profit? This was a total waste of time. I never received my $100 back either.*

Impersonation of the Other Party

Scammers sometimes watch high value auctions, then impersonate the seller. Since eBay has started hiding the identities of bidders this has not been a problem. These crooks will email the buyer telling them they are the seller and their email is not working so they are 'resending' the information. The new information has a new PayPal payment address or new mailing address for payments. If the buyer is fooled, they may send payment to the wrong person. EBay has started hiding the identities of high bidders for high value items to stop this type of fraud. Make sure you use the eBay Mesages Center to contact the seller. The seller should have the auction setup to make instant payments at auction close which will also avoid this scam.

Middleman Scam

An item sells for a high price. A scammer contacts the buyer pretending to be seller and contacts seller pretending to be buyer. The scammer claims their(buyer or seller) email is not working and gives a new email address. They then ask the buyer to send payment to them instead of the real seller. At the same time they assure the seller payment is on the way to prevent the seller from trying to contact the buyer directly. They may even send counterfeit payment to the seller and attempt to obtain the product and the real payment. This keeps the real buyer and seller from contacting each other until the scam is complete.

DECEPTIVE TITLES

Titles that do not list the item are a violation of eBay rules. You must list the item being sold in the title. Beware of any seller who offers an item, but does not state what the item is in the title, or if they use words like 'banned' or 'illegal' in the title, or if the title clearly uses keyword spamming. Sellers who use sales pitches or enticing come-on's in the title instead of the item description should be avoided. Scammers often use this technique by listing adult oriented auctions with alluring titles that do not describe what is being sold along with a gallery image of a scantily clad girl.

The seller may use the auction to lure victims into their trap. They may have a phone number to call or an email address or otherwise will try to contact the buyer and offer to sell some desirable item at a great price. Once the seller has the buyer's credit card or other personal information, they never hear from the seller again. Such auctions should be reported to eBay. Titles that do not describe the item being sold are common signs of fraudulent sellers.

Some intelligent scammers have taken a new approach to keyword spamming. They combine a knock-off product along with a designer product sample. This keeps them in compliance with eBay rules, but just barely. They will obtain the free samples of designer cologne or lotion and give them away with the fake item.

Polo Black Calfskin Sandal

This title appears to offer a black Polo sandal, but it may actually go to an auction offering generic look-alike women's sandals with a free sample of Polo Black brand cologne.

THIRD PARTY CHECKS

A third party check is a check that is not from the person you are selling to. If John Smith won your auction, then why is he sending you a check from Jane Doe? Why can John Smith not open his own bank account? Never accept third party checks from anyone for anything. Third party checks are common sources of fraud. Family member fraud is a common source of third party checks. Beware of someone's brother writing a check on his account to pay for your auctioned item. If he does not have his own bank account, then there is a reason for it. You do not want to do business with him.

PICK-UP FRAUD

Sellers who sell large and expensive items can be the target of Pick-Up Fraud. The dishonest buyer will pay by PayPal, arrange to pick up the item in person and then file for a reversal with PayPal because they know the seller cannot provide tracking information. When a PayPal payment is made, the buyer has the option to not include their address. Normally the buyers address is listed in the confirmation email and in your PayPal account for the shipping address. Beware of PayPal payments that do not include the buyers address. The buyer is hiding their address from you.

Dishonest buyers can also use counterfeit cashier's checks or money orders for this fraud scheme. You can use the eBay option to "Request Personal Information" for the buyer, however if the account was hijacked or the buyer simply lied during sign-up, this information may not be helpful. It is best to accept cash on pickup only.

Contact Me First

Any seller who states in the auction that the bidder must contact them before bidding is attempting to sell outside of eBay. Scammers will hijack user accounts and then post fake auctions that require bidders to contact the alleged seller before bidding. When any potential bidder emails or calls the phone number in the auction, the alleged seller offers to sell the item at a great price and may even offer free shipping. This is a common scam. Never trust a seller who wants buyers to contact him before bidding.

Some high value auctions do require bidder pre-approval. This will show "Bidder pre-approval required" in the top information section of the auction. The seller must add the bidder to an approved list. This reduces the number of fraudulent bids on high priced items.

Legitimate sellers using bidder pre-approval will add bidders to the approved list and never attempt to sell outside of eBay. If you receive a second chance offer even though your bid was third or fourth highest at auction close, it is a scam. Any auction for a low priced item that requires bidder pre-approval is a scam. Legitimate sellers do not use bid pre-approval on low priced items(under $2000 usually). Any auction claiming the seller has a Buy-It-Now price, which does not actually have a Buy-It-Now option, is a sign the seller is attempting to sell outside of eBay. Never trust such sellers.

Help Me Sell

More accurately, help me steal. Beware of anyone who asks you to sell something for them on eBay. Scammers will post to classifieds and message boards asking for help selling items on eBay. They will then ask victims to post expensive items and to let the scammer know when they are sold. The victim then sends the payment to the scammer and keeps a percentage as instructed by the scammer. The scammer disappears, leaving the eBay members high and dry with no items to ship. This same type of scam occurs when criminals claim to be Drop Shippers seeking sellers to re-sell goods on eBay. The common thread is promising '*all you have to do is sell and I will pay you*'. These are always scams. Beware of any stranger who wants you to sell anything for them on eBay.

You cannot use your PayPal account to transfer money to someone you are selling items for anyway. PayPal accounts cannot be used to transfer money for other people. Doing so can be considered the crime of Money Laundering.

International Electronics Sales

Only ship expensive electronics to the USA(if you are in the USA yourself) or Canada and unselect International shipping for your shipping options. International orders for expensive electronics are frequently fraudulent. International buyers will use stolen credit cards or hijacked PayPal accounts to pay for expensive electronics. There is no reason to sell expensive electronics outside of the USA. International buyers can purchase locally or from local eBay sellers. Any price benefit is erased by shipping.

Beware of buying laptops or other expensive electronics from sellers outside of the USA. These items are more expensive in other parts of the world, not less expensive. You will never receive a good deal unless it is a scam. Buyers outside of the USA buy expensive electronics from the USA, they do not sell them to the USA unless they are gray market, counterfeit, stolen, or do not exist.

Overpayment

Some scammers will purchase an expensive item and send payment for more than the value. They will purchase a car for $4500 and then send payment for $14,500 and claim there was a mistake. They may send a counterfeit cashier's check or a use the fake wire transfer technique. The scammer can mail a counterfeit check for deposit to the victim's local bank. They will ask that it be deposited to the victim's account using the information provided for the money transfer. There was no actual wire transfer. When the victim looks at their online statement, it will show a deposit for $14,500. This is not real money. This is only the account showing a counterfeit check was deposited and the bank has credited it to the victim's account. The victim will think a wire transfer has been made. The scammer will then ask the victim to wire back the over payment and keep the amount they owe. This is a scam 100% of the time. No one sends a payment for more than the value of the item. When the victim wires the $10,000 'back' to the scammer, the scammer takes the money and runs. The original payment is returned as counterfeit and the victim's bank account no longer shows the $14,500 deposit. Now the account is $10,000 negative. The victim owes the bank money. No one will ever overpay for an auction like this. The amount could just as easily have been a $1000 scam as a $10,000 scam. If anyone ever makes a large purchase from you and then sends more than the amount requested, contact the police and your bank.

Multiple PayPal Payments

Never accept multiple Paypal payments for an item. Small time scammers who are using their own Payapl account will split payments and send part of the auction payment the day of the auction, then send the rest from his or her own account for the rest of the payment. They will receive the item and then file a reversal on the second payment or both. Now, the seller has two transactions but only one tracking/delivery confirmation number so one of the transactions will be reversed. Any buyer who sends two payments instead of one is a scammer. No buyer ever has a legitimate reason to send two Paypal payments. If they send two payments and they come from two different accounts, then it should be obvious they are a scammer who has hijacked multiple accounts.

eBay Message Boards

EBay provides forums or message boards for users. There are scammers pretending to be eBay or Paypal employees who will offer to resolve your problems, undo reversals, or provide information on other members who have committed scams. These people are lying and are trying to scam you. They will try to obtain your information, your login ID and password as well as credit card numbers and other information while claiming they must charge a fee or must verify you are the real owner of the account(so they ask for the password).

Take Advantage of Me

I dont know too much about jewelry so I am setting the by now price at $150 for this waitch. It says rolex on the face and works good.

If it sounds too good to be true. It is. Scammers often use the *take advantage of me* psychology to attract victims. The bidder thinks he can take advantage of someone and obtain a great bargain. In the end, it is the scammer who has the advantage. The buyer also is unlikely to file for a refund or file a fraud claim because the buyer knows he did something unethical in trying to take advantage of a seller.

EBay motors is a favorite place for scammers. This is where the high priced items are and that always attracts criminals.

If you are selling a vehicle on eBay Motors, select the option to block international bidders. You will never sell a vehicle to a legitimate international buyer. If you are selling a common vehicle then no international buyer would seriously consider paying real money for it. It is much cheaper to purchase locally plus there are many import and export regulations involved and it is expensive. Individuals do not import/export vehicles like this.

The scammer will try to use one of the previously described cashier's check or wire transfer scams. Buyers looking for expensive sports cars or specialty vehicles will buy them locally or use an import company that specializes in such vehicles. You will never sell a vehicle to a legitimate international buyer.

Never purchase a vehicle on eBay Motors without first obtaining the VIN and checking the vehicle history. Be sure to check the vehicle history through carfax.com to see if it matches the current seller's location. Some dishonest sellers will copy VIN information from other auctions. Also verify the VIN on the vehicle you receive is the same as the one you expected. If it is different, the seller has pulled the old switch-a-roo.

Beware of salvage vehicles being sold as good new or used vehicles. After any flood or hurricane, there are many new car lots that have flooded vehicles. These are sold to liquidators or auction companies that resell them. The buyers also purchase wrecked cars that are written off as totaled. Sometimes they will take a car involved in a front end collision and another that was involved in a rear end collision, cut the vehicles in half and weld the good parts together.

The buyers clean them up and repair the vehicles before having them re-titled in a state that will not show the SALVAGED designation on the title. These vehicles are generally unsafe and plagued with problems. A flooded vehicle may run, but it also may have many hidden problems. These are commonly sold on eBay as new and good used vehicles without anyone revealing they are salvaged.

There is a much more detailed report on eBay vehicle fraud available from http://Bonus.DontBidOnIt.com as part of the eBay Mastery Course.

Auction Consistency

Check a sellers past auctions for consistency before purchasing. A seller may offer some used hunting equipment, a truck part, and a sleeping bag. That seems normal. A seller offering a genuine Gucci handbag, and a real Rolex watch, and ten other auctions for generic white tube socks and a CD of the 80's greatest hits is not normal. Anyone who could purchase a genuine Guicci handbag and a Rolex watch would not bother selling tube socks or care about the $3 they might receive for an old music CD. This seller does not make sense at all. The items are either stolen or counterfeit.

Also watch for sellers claiming they are selling a personal item who actually have ten auctions for the same item. No seller has a collection of ten Gucci handbags in their closet. If they do, they are not concerned about selling them on eBay.

NAME VARIATIONS

The name of the person you are doing business with should be consistent. If their eBay ID shows one name, and their email another, and they want a payment sent to a third name, something is wrong.

An eBay id that contradicts the email addresses indicates a scammer who has hijacked someone's eBay account and is redirecting contact to the scammer's email address. Beware of someone using an email service in one country while claiming to be in another. Not everyone uses their name in their eBay ID or email, but if they do, it is a good cross check.

Use common sense comparisons when dealing with buyer information. Does their eBay ID, email address, and ship-to name match?

Are these members legitimate?

 EBay ID   Email Address   Name
tom-at-ebay123456   tomsmith@dontbidonit.com   Tom Smith
     Yes, all of the names match, we are dealing with Tom.
tom-at-ebay123456   fjlsj$100@dontbidonit.com   Will Doe
     No, random email, no name match, this does not look right.
tom-at-ebay123456   marysmith$1@dontbidonit.com Raji Nespela
     No, the names do not match, one is for Tom, another is for
     Mary and the third is Raji, there is something wrong with
     this buyer or seller and they do not look legitimate.

SELL TO ME NOW

The seller receives a pleading message:

Please end the auction and relist with a fixed price Buy-It-Now so I can buy now. Please it is so important to me. I urgently need this item and I am unemployed so I cannot wait until the end of the auction or buy from another seller.

The scam buyer nags incessantly until the seller relents and agrees to sell to them at a fixed price. When the seller cancels the item and relists, the buyer disappears and never bids. Now the seller is stuck with the extra fees for the cancelled auction and may have to relist again as a regular auction because the agreed price may be above market price. That means the seller is out a third set of listing fees. This is not a scam for money. It is an ego trip for the fake bidder. They have fraudulently conned an innocent seller into cancelling an auction the bidder had no intention of bidding on.

Sometimes the buyers claim they want the item at above market price, sometimes they give a sad and false story to obtain the item at lower than market price. I had a fake buyer like this try to con me into ending an auction early. I told him he was welcome to bid and I would not end the auction early. He replied with a not so nice message, very agitated that I would not take a $50 hit and sell the item for half it's value.

Any bidder who asks you to cancel an auction and relist so they can buy now is a fraudulent bidder. Psychologically normal people simply do not make requests like this. Honest bidders will place their bid and wait for the auction to close so everyone a fair chance to bid.

Fake Buyer Phishing

Fake Buyer Phishing occurs when the scammer purchases an expensive item from a seller and then tries to pump the seller for personal information. The buyer has no interest in the item and no intent to pay.

The buyer may request the sellers name, phone number and address just to 'verify' they are legitimate before sending payment. It is common for scammers to try and put honest sellers on the defensive by implying they may not be who they claim. People tend to give out more information than they should when they are on the defensive. The buyer will then respond and requests more of the seller's personal information. In follow up emails they will request more and more information to 'verify' the seller is legitimate. Each time they promise to pay by PayPal or other instant means, but they always have some reason for a delay or claiming they need information for the money transfer. This is nothing more than a scam to obtain information so the scammer can steal the seller's identity. It is identify theft.

The scammer may even send fake email messages that appear to be from eBay saying the buyer has filed a complaint and they are requesting verification information. Any replies go to the scammer.

My _____ Is Not Working

Scammers frequently use the excuse of '*email not working*' to redirect communications to a different email address. Beware of anyone who says their email, PayPal account, or anything else is not working.

Beware of anyone who begins communicating with one address then requests to change to a different address. Scammers often have email or PayPal accounts disabled and have to change them frequently. If you are contacted by someone who says their email account is disabled or not working and they provide a different account with completely different contact information, you are communicating with a scammer. No one has an msn.com email address one day and a hotmail.com address the next.

Do not send a PayPal payment to any seller who claims to be "having problems." Avoid anyone who claims their PayPal account is not working and wants you to send payment through "a friend's" PayPal account. Scammers hijack other people's accounts and often want to send payment from one account while having the goods sent to another name and address. This is always a warning sign.

Newbie Fraud

This is not exactly a scam in itself, but a method criminals use to find marks. Criminals look for sellers with low feedback scores who appear to be legitimate sellers(not other scammers). The scammers target people who are unfamiliar with eBay rules and unfamiliar with how PayPal works. The scammer will make an outside of eBay transaction offer or bid on the newbies auction and then send a fake PayPal confirmation email. They may also send a fake eBay email saying the payment has been received and will be released when tracking information is provided or some similar scam. Inexperienced members may ship the goods, to someone they should not. Criminals want to take advantage of people who are unfamiliar with PayPal or eBay.

Most of the brand name counterfeit clothing on eBay is, well, as I said, counterfeit. Anyone offering a large number of a single item like expensive designer jeans or re-listing a single designer item over and over is almost always selling counterfeits. No one has a garage full of real designer jeans they are willing to sell for half price. If they do have a garage full of real designer jeans, they are stolen. You can look at items the seller has previously sold to see their history. Are they selling this same item over and over? Do they seem to have an unusual number of high end designer items? Do they ship from New York or Los Angeles? Those are counterfeit distribution capitols. Do they have no previous sales or a zero feedback account? All of these are warning signs. Counterfeits are of poor quality and buying stolen items is not a good idea. The people selling these are criminals. You do not want to give your personal information, check numbers, credit card numbers, or any other information to them. You never know who they will sell your information to. You certainly do not want to send them a Western Union payment. You will never see your money again. Sorry, you will not find a great deal on new designer clothing unless it is stolen or counterfeit.

Check the item location. You will never purchase legitimate designer items from Asia, South America, or Mexico. Many Asian counterfeiters either falsely claim to be in Europe or Canada, or use distributors in these countries. They can also use distributors in the USA. This is how some people wind up with a garage full of counterfeit designer jeans.

By the way, no one is fooled by cheap counterfeits. Do you really want your friends to complement your nice new designer handbag and then look at each other and snicker when your back is turned over the obvious counterfeit? Save up and buy the real thing. There are legitimate used designer items on eBay.

A seller may have found an item on sale at a high end store. They may have used a gift certificate to buy the item. The seller may have bought the item and decided to sell it before her husband sees it. Ask questions if you are unsure. Auctions claiming to be high end designer 'authorized resellers' are selling counterfeits. Many designers have sales restrictions which do not allow their items to be sold through eBay.

Beware of anyone selling a designer item who does not show photos of the actual item. If they are using images from the designers website or an image that comes up in a Google search, you can be certain the seller is a scammer offering either nothing or counterfeit goods.

Authenticity cards are easily faked. They may not have the fancy holograms, but the fakes can appear real if you have nothing to compare them to. Receipts and other paperwork can be easily faked.

No seller on eBay is an authorized reseller for any big name designer. Beware of sellers offering big name designer items and claiming "I am an authorized seller". How are they authorized? Can they prove it? It makes no difference because big name designers do not sell their items through mom and pop outlets. They only sell to large distributors who deal directly with large high end stores like Dillard's or Macy's.

High end designers do not sell seconds. They are high end brands. They do not pollute their product lines with damaged goods.

There are some clear warning signs in auctions offering brand name items at good prices.

This item was created for Europe(or any other area/country) so it is a little different than the US version.
         or
We can only ship to Japan(or any other area/country).

Very few designers create different items for different countries. There are very few designers who create special low-end versions for other countries and those that do, never allow the foreign versions to be sold outside of those areas. Any seller posting an auction for designer merchandise and then claiming they only ship to one country is lying. They intend to ship anywhere anyone will pay. That is assuming they plan to ship anything.

This wholesale item might be slightly different than the store version.

Why would the wholesale version be different from the store version? It is the same item. Designers do not make different versions for different stores or distribution channels. Another sign of a counterfeit.

These have no tags.
         or
Tags will be removed before shipping.
         or
Tags were removed for (insert any fake reason here).
         or
These are samples and have no tags.

No tags on a new designer item means they are fakes. Why would a shipper of a new item bother to remove tags? Major department stores require a sales receipt so removing the tags has nothing to do with a return. Department stores do not remove tags when they sell an item. They may cut the tag in half, but they never remove it. This is a clear sign of a counterfeit. This often means the seller was too lazy to Photoshop out the tags from the stock photo they stole from the designer's website. Many designer tags have counterfeit proof elements like holograms which are expensive to duplicate. This is why tags are not included on counterfeit. No tags=Fake.

I can't guarantee authenticity.

This means "*It's fake but I don't want to admit it*" This item may be a counterfeit or a generic look-alike the seller is trying to pass off as a designer brand.

Unfortunately many people who buy these high end brand names have no idea what the real thing looks like. They receive the cheap counterfeit and leave positive feedback raving about their purchase. Some know they are counterfeit, but do not care. They do not realize they paid $200 for a handbag that cost $5 to manufacture and will fall apart in a couple of months.

There are legitimate and semi-legitimate listings for designer clothing. Some of the items are listed as new, but they are in fact used. No tags can indicate a used item if it is from a seller who does not usually sell high end designer items.

Designer labels and insignia can be purchased in bulk. Sometimes these can be purchased from vendors on the streets in New York along with a $10 Rolex. Some sellers purchase these labels and glue or sew them into generic-look alike garments to pass them off as genuine. This is why Izod stopped using stick on aligators. People would purchase the counterfeit emblems and glue them to shirts.

Too Much Personal Information

Beware of anyone who sends you too much personal information. If someone contacts you and explains who they are, what they do, and where they live, they are trying to scam you. Normal people do not contact a stranger and explain their life story.

> **Anyone who gives too much personal information is trying to commit fraud.**
>
> *My name is Mr. Bandai and I am in Nigeria, I am the STATE MINISTER for the GOVERNMENT OF NIGERIA, and I have recently had to go to a divorce so I must sell my favorite possessions that I have had in my family for many years.*
>
> *or*
>
> *..my husband has died and these things remind me of him. He was the Finance Minister here and I worked as his secretary for the last ten years. This experience has been most difficult on me. I hope you can help. I need someone to buy them. I have nothing because his children have taken everything and all my accounts are frozen until the details are straight with my bank. Please find in your heart to ship to me the payment quickly so I can resume my life and I will post your purchase items quickly.*

Cashier's Checks

Cashier's checks should be verified with the issuing bank or you should hold the item until the check clears before you release the goods. If the buyer demands you ship sooner, don't make plans for the money you received because the check will be returned. If the buyer picks up an expensive item in person, you should make them wait while you call the issuing bank. Don't use the phone number on the check either. Call information for the bank number. If they conveniently arrange the pickup outside of banking hours, ask for their drivers license number and write it, along with their name and address on the check or take a photo of the license. Compare the person on the license to the person claiming to be the license owner. If they do not look like the person in the photo, excuse yourself to go to the bathroom and call the police. If you are selling a vehicle and you do not ask for the person's license, you could be liable if they have a wreck and are unlicensed. You just sold a car to an unlicensed driver. Take a photo of the person by the car if you can. Call the police if they refuse to let you see their ID. If you are selling a vehicle, arrange to meet in the bank parking lot. Never meet anyone alone. Always have a friend with you even if they wait in the car where they can watch and hear what is happening. You never want to show up alone and find out the buyer brought two friends. If the buyer shows up with their family, it does not make them more trustworthy either.

Once you are at the bank with your friend and you have the check, you can then have the bank verify the check. If the buyer does not want to meet at a location with security then consider that a warning sign. This is a common type of fraud which is used to steal cars.

Beware of people giving advice on message boards. They rarely know what they are talking about. Sometimes their advice may be against eBay or PayPal rules. Sometimes it violates the law. When someone gives advice in a chat room or on a message board, especially on the eBay community boards, you should make sure it is good advice before trying it. Some people have an idea then post it as if they have been doing it for years. In fact, they have never tried it.

Some of this advice is posted by scammers. They recommend fraudulent escrow services, fraudulent drop shipping services or other schemes in chat rooms or message boards.

In the eBay community boards, you can find many posts by people with zero or even negative ratings giving advice. These people have no business advising others how to protect themselves from scams or how to buy or sell. These people should not be giving any advice because they have no eBay experience. Many of the zero and negative feedback people posting recommendations and giving advice are scammers. Some scammers post *buyer's guides* to the eBay Forums that recommend a product or makes the seller sound legitimate. This leads inexperienced members to viewing the scammer's auctions.

Beware of eBay advice from friends. When someone receives their first gold star, after 10 positive feedbacks, they think they are an expert and begin giving advice. They may be repeating something they saw on a message board that was posted by a scammer.

> *Go to this auction 19019301 and contact the seller, he will sell direct for half price but he only has ten left.*
>
> *justgotscammedonebay(0) writes:*
> *I just used scam-me-escrow.com and they are great, I should receive my car in a few weeks*
>
> *I was just reading on a message board that Western Union is the safest way to send auciton payments....*
>
> *I dont know what this guy is complaining about...I have used scam-me drop shipping...and they are the best...everyone should sign up with them...*

UPGRADE SCAM

A bidder wins a digital camera and then complains the item is not as described, or is scratched or non working. The seller offers a refund and the buyer returns the camera. When the seller receives the returned camera, it is clearly heavily used and scratched up. The seller received a different camera than the one he shipped.

The buyer wanted a free upgrade and purchased an identical item on eBay hoping to return his bad or worn out old item. Make sure you record the serial number or photograph the serial number of expensive items before shipping.

My Shipper Scam

Beware of any buyer who wants to purchase a large item using their own shipping service to ship to themselves in another country. No one uses *their own* shipping service. A legitimate shipping service has a name, a website, a telephone listing, a business license.

This scam commonly targets people selling industrial equipment and pinball games. No one in a foreign country is going to buy a large tractor plow, then pay to have it shipped. It is not worth the cost of the shipping.

Scammers use 'my own shipper' to make the transaction sound easy. A person has a large item that would be difficult to ship and out of nowhere comes a buyer who is willing to pickup the item. The buyer is almost always in a big rush and needs the item urgently. Instead of purchasing the same item locally for less than it would cost to ship your item, they want to send an anonymous shipping company to pickup the item. The scammer will then send a counterfeit money order or counterfeit cashier's check for more than the amount due. The victim is told to send the extra amount to the 'freight company'.

Once the victim deposits the cashier's check and sends the shipping payment to the fictional shipping company by Western Union, they never hear from the buyer again. The cashier's check is returned as counterfeit and the victim's checking account is debited the full amount. The victim now owes the bank a returned check fee, plus the value of the original cashier's check. No shipping company will ever show up and someone in Romania or Nigerian officials have agreements not to interfere with the organizations that run these scams which makes them all a little richer each day.

Power Seller/Verified Scam

There are techniques for anyone to become a Power Seller. Anyone with a stolen identity and credit report can become ID Verified. Anyone can join the Square Trade program. These icons in an auction do not by themselves mean the person is trustworthy. The account could still have been hijacked by a scammer, or a scammer may have taken the extra time and effort needed to add these icons to their fraudulent account. Do not trust a member simply because they have some fancy icons by their name that say they are trustworthy.

There are techniques to buy your way into Power Seller status without selling a single legitimate item. Scammers can create an account, use the Power Seller methods to become a Power Seller, then wait three months for the Power Seller invitation. Then they begin the real scams. There are also people who create Power Seller ID's and sell them to others.

An icon saying someone is trustworthy does not make them trustworthy. A new user who has a Power Seller icon, an ID Verify icon, and a Square Trade notice in their auctions, is less trustworthy. Why would a new member need so much *validation*? This member has gone overboard to obtain credibility and is therefore suspect.

Get Rich Quick Scams

There are many auctions showing a photo of a guy in a suit, knee deep in cash, often with a half naked girl hanging on his shoulder and the caption says "I Made A Zillion Dollars in Ten Minutes" or similar nonsense. All you have to do is buy their eBook, or program they printed out on their printer and bound at the local copy shop for $19.95. Make money selling eBooks, trading stocks, selling web templates, selling vitamins, drop-shipping, work-at-home. These are all scams.

The money is in selling a dream to people for $9.99 or $19.95. These scams often point to other pay websites which the author also owns where you have to buy your products, pay for mentoring, or some other whacky service.

> *Although it is not on eBay, one of my favorites is the TV commercial where the woman says "I made over a million dollars!" then on the screen it says "in the past 9 years" Nine years? If your business only grosses one million dollars in nine years, you have wasted your time.*

The advice in these Get Rich eBooks is often very general and sometimes downright false. These eBooks may recommend fraudulent escrow services controlled by the seller or a fraudulent drop shipping company.

Many ebooks give bad advice or impossible advice. If you want to be rich, buy up land in Russia. OK, what land, where, who do I talk to, how do I know if it is a good deal. When do I sell it? These books never give the details. If the author knew the details, they would be doing it and not selling a cheap eBook telling others how to do it.

Anyone who made enough money on eBay to buy a car or a house, or a waist high pile of cash, does not sell eBooks for 99 cents.

You will never 'get rich quick'. Making money is a process that starts slow and builds. If you are really interested in business, buy some legitimate books by known authors. You can often pick them up used at Amazon for pennies.

How I made over $2000 in just 10 days using a ridiculously stupid technique I borrowed...

This should be an obvious scam on eBay or outside of eBay.

Unfamiliar Auction Payment Services

Scammers use unfamiliar payment services to trick sellers into thinking payments have been made that have not been made or to trick buyers into revealing their credit card number or PayPal information or other financial information.

The winner of your auction tells you he wants to use an unfamiliar system such as AuctionPay, which is a legitimate service. You receive an email stating the payment was made and Wells Fargo is holding the money until you can provide a tracking number. The expectation is to ship the item to obtain a tracking number. The email is fake and has nothing to do with Wells Fargo's AuctionPay service. The scammer sent the forged email in an attempt to trick the seller into shipping the goods. The seller is unfamiliar with how AuctionPay works and may ship in good faith so he can provide a tracking number to release their funds. Once the seller ships, he never receives any payment.

PYRAMID SCHEMES

Any auction that offers a popular item at a super discount price, but says you must sign up other people is a scam. This is called a Pyramid Scheme. Some pyramid schemes sound great but the rules are structured such that no one can ever obtain the promised prize. You, or your friends, must purchase other unrelated items to obtain points. No one can obtain enough points or for other reasons they cannot claim the points they have acquired.

Some of these schemes are not technically pyramid schemes, but when you have to explain the difference....

Some involve signing up for free trials for services or magazines. You must then cancel the services in 45 days or you will be billed automatically. If these schemes are run by reputable companies they can be legitimate and in the end you may receive a free iPod or whatever other product they are promoting.

When a legitimate company offers something, like free iPods, there will also be scammers setting up look-alike sites offering similar services that only collect personal information. They can use eBay to advertise and promote their sites.

Some sellers on eBay take advantage of ignorance and try to re-sell this scheme to others. They charge others who become one of their sign-ups, helping the seller to gain their free item. This is not a scam that appeals to organized crime. This appeals to teenagers and dishonest individuals who want something for nothing.

A Google search will usually reveal the original website that offers the real service so you never have to pay for the scheme listed on eBay. Pyramid schemes are sometimes cloaked using the name Buyer's Club on eBay. The seller's don't want to call it a Pyramid scheme in the title for obvious reasons.

CHARITY AUCTIONS

EBay has rules against offering unauthorized charity auctions. The only legitimate charity auctions are run through MissionFish
http://www.missionfish.org MissionFish charges your credit card the donated amount of their fee and passes the rest to your charity.

EBAY SAFE PAYMENT SCAM

ebay-escrow.com, safe-harbor-escrow.com ebayescro.cn, paypal-escrow.com paypal-escrow-services.hk, western-union-escrow.com, ebay-securepayments.com, paypal-premium-services.com paypal-instantpay.com

These are scammers, all of them. Scammers frequently register domains with names that make them look official. These domains may look real but they are fake. Any buyer or seller who asks you to use a 'Safe Payment Program' or any secure payment method that appears to be linked to a large company is planning to scam you.

Any alleged payment service that emails claiming it will release the funds when you provide a tracking number is a fraud.

WAIT A LITTLE LONGER

When a credit card is used to pay for a PayPal transaction and a chargeback is filed for unauthorized use, it can take up to 30 days before the owner contacts the credit card company, and another 30 days before the credit card company sends their notice to PayPal and possibly another 30 days before PayPal notifies the seller. After 90 days, the Postal Inspectors will no longer investigate mail fraud because the paper trail is gone. The criminals want to stretch out the complaint process as long as possible.

Act swiftly if you suspect fraud. Never ship to an address or name different from the one on the paypal account notice and never ship to c/o one person at a different address.

Any buyer who promises repeatedly to make a bad transaction right and asks the seller to wait a little longer is trying to pull a scam. Any seller who claims they are having trouble shipping and asks for another few days and then another few days is trying to pull a scam.

The buyer may have sent a bad check, filed a false credit card chargeback or used some other way of reversing the payment. The dishonest seller is only trying to buy more time to either wait out the buyer until they give up or until the seller can scam more people before moving to a new account.

Sometimes the scammer disappears, but if their hijacked accounts or created accounts are still working, they will attempt to appease any upset sellers or buyers and string them along for as long as possible.

This scam does not require a stolen credit card. A dishonest buyer who decides they want to keep their item and the money can file a chargeback on their own card while telling the seller it is all a mistake. They may claim their spouse filed the chargeback without them knowing and to be patient and they will take care of everything. They are lying. The buyer may even say to ignore the chargeback. In the meantime, the clock is ticking and they only have to stretch the situation out until they can no longer be prosecuted. If the seller ignores the chargeback or does not respond to the PayPal notice, the charge will be automatically reversed because the seller did not respond in the specified time.

If you think someone is trying to drag out the process and delay you from acting, ACT FAST! File a PayPal complaint if your shipper is making excuses. File a criminal complaint and contact the Postal Inspectors if you paid for an item by mail or shipped an item and the payment bounced or was reversed. Do not wait.

FAKE DELIVERY CONFIRMATION

The dishonest seller receives a PayPal payment and then ships junk mail(or an empty envelope) to the buyer with delivery confirmation. The buyer receives junk mail and throws it in the trash without paying attention to it. The buyer files a PayPal complaint for non receipt. Then the seller proves receipt using the delivery confirmation number.

The seller sent junk mail knowing the buyer would throw it away without looking at it. Now the seller has a delivery confirmation number to prove they shipped the goods when they in fact shipped nothing. The postal clerk should really question why someone is re-shipping junk mail using delivery confirmation, but they cannot do much about it anyway. Shipping junkmail is not a crime.

DISCOUNT COUPONS

20% of Dell XPS desktop with minimum purchase of $999 Buy-It-Now $10.00

Some sellers offer discount coupons which are codes entered during checkout at major shopping sites. The seller emails a special code the buyer can use when purchasing from the legitimate website to receive a discount. These are from reputable companies like Dell Computers, Amazon, and Lowes. The sellers are taking advantage of buyer ignorance or laziness. These coupon codes are frequently part of advertising campaigns which are widely distributed. Sometimes the company posts the code to their own website.

There is no physical coupon so the sellers of these coupon codes can sell them over and over.

There is no reason to pay for a coupon code that is posted on the Internet for free. There are specialty websites that track coupon codes and post them for their members. 4computercoupons.com, dealcatcher.com, couponmountain.com. You can also Google for coupon codes and find them on message boards.

5% Discount Coupon for Air Mattress Bed - Buy It Now $1.00

Some discount coupons are for unknown companies. These are actually advertising schemes. The companies raise their prices $100 then offer a $100 off coupon on eBay. People who never would have visited the company website might buy a $1 coupon with the promise of saving $100 which then results in a large sale to the company. Many of these listings are actually nothing more than commercials. When the auction loads, an automatic commercial begins playing with a sales pitch for the product the coupon is for. They are not selling the coupon, the coupon is a come-on to lead people into listening to or watching their commercial. They are basically using eBay for advertising.

It is hard to call this a true scam, but I guess I just did.

AFRICAN RESELLER SCAM

I am a store operator here in Africa and I have found your product sells very well here. I would like to make a large deal to purchase many of your item quickly.

You will never have a 'product' that sells well in Africa especially Nigeria. This scam involves a scammer pretending to be interested in some product you offer through eBay. Most of the time it is clear the scammer does not even know what your product is or what it is for. They always want to make a large transaction and they want to do it fast. The remainder of the scam can vary. They may want the victim to send them money first for 'customs fees' or they may send a counterfeit cashiers check for more than the amount due and ask the remainder be returned by Western Union. Sometimes they send a fake email that appears to be from Western Union or PayPal claiming you have been paid and you should ship the goods immediately.

As an individual, you will never conduct any legitimate business with anyone in Nigeria. This simply will not happen in your lifetime.

Scammers go where the money is. The big money is in vehicles and real estate on eBay. The same scams that work elsewhere work in the Real Estate area. There are a number of things you can do to protect yourself from Real Estate Fraud.

Call the County Clerk's Office at the County Court House where the property is located. They can provide the name and contact information for the owner, the real owner. If the name is not the same as the person who is selling the property, you need to ask for a notarized Power of Attorney or an Agency Agreement(in the case of a real estate company) which will state that the person selling the property is acting on behalf of and with the permission of the property owner.

It is possible to look up information on the web regarding ownership information, but this information is not always accurate. Scammers can also setup fake sites which list only the properties they claim to own. Beware of any seller who points you to a specific site that contains information that cannot be verified with the County Clerk's office.

A Warranty Deed, Land Contract or any other document that transfers property ownership must be on file with the County Clerk. If it is not on file, it is not legally binding. If a seller claims to have any ownership instrument like this, request that they record it with the County Clerk's office and state you will not send payment until it is duly recorded. If the seller balks, they are trying to scam you. Legitimate sellers have no problem recording legitimate paperwork.

Beware of anyone who wants to transfer property using a Quit Claim Deed. These deeds can be purchased in any office supply store. They are commonly used to steal property.

Beware of any property with a UCC(Uniform Commercial Code) attachment or lien. This means someone has a claim on the property other than the owner and they can take ownership ahead of you if the property is transferred. You would not receive a refund either.

Beware of anyone who wants to do anything unusual. Provide unusual paperwork, do anything in a non-standard way, avoid escrow.

Anyone who wants to sell property will go through the legal channels and transfer the deed using a lawyer and the Court House. Beware of anyone who requests unusual transfers.

Watch for signs that the seller is not a resident of the area where the land is being sold. They may use a mailbox service that forwards their mail or a PO box and file a forwarding order to have their mail sent to them. Make sure you know where the seller is physically located.

Beware of cheap lots. I would be glad to sell you a gorgeous ocean view lot on the coast of California; cheap too. Many people would. These lots are too small for a septic tank or they are solid rock therefore a house cannot be built on them. They are so remote or in such a rocky location that no one could build on them anyway. The photos may look great, but they may or may not be the actual property. Even if the photos are the real property, they cannot show what property access looks like.

Contact the Zoning Commission for the city/county and explain that you are looking at purchasing the land, but you needed to ask them what restrictions are on the lot. If you want to build on the property, ask about the septic tank restrictions. Even if the seller says they already checked and it was allowed to install a septic system, check anyway. If the seller is a scammer, they have every reason to lie.

Sometimes just asking is not enough. If the office is not familiar with the lot, they may say it can have a septic system, but their story may change when they inspect it. If you want to build a house, the lot must be Pre-Approved for a septic system. Any good seller would have already obtained this pre-approval because they would know it was necessary to sell the lot at a good price.

Never buy a building you plan to use without hiring a licensed inspector for a pre-closing inspection. Any seller who objects to an inspection is trying to scam you.

Beware of any seller who is offering property they have not seen or property they do not have pictures of. These are especially lazy scammers because they have not bothered to steal photos from past auctions.

Visit the property. It does not matter if it is a house, an apartment building, or an empty lot, there is nothing like seeing it for yourself. Is it worth a $1000 round trip flight to avoid being scammed out of $30,000 or more?

If you are not experienced with property transfers, HIRE AN ATTORNEY! They are expensive, but they can also save you a lot of headaches. If the seller backs out or stops communicating when you ask to have your attorney handle the transfer, you know it is a scam.

Do not trust your attorney! You cannot throw a printout of the auction on your attorney's desk and expect them to tell you if this is a scam or not. When you finish this book you will know more about eBay scams than your attorney. Do your own research too.

Pre Paid Shipping

Companies often provide their shipping numbers for FedEx or UPS to suppliers in order to ship items. They do this to pay shipping and avoid the '& Handling' fees. It is not appropriate to even ask a seller on eBay to ship using your account. Shipping quotes on eBay include shipping and handling. If a seller uses another persons account, they are begin cheated out of their handling fees which were a legal part of the auction contract.

Scammers will buy an expensive item on eBay and ask that it be shipped to their work address. They then provide their work FedEx or UPS shipping number to use. The scammer may also send a pre-paid shipping label. After the seller ships, the PayPal transaction is reversed. The scammer used a stolen credit card or hijacked PayPal account and a stolen shipper account number. Now the seller has no proof of delivery because they shipped to a different address. The seller has lost the item and the money.

Only ship to the PayPal Verified Address. Buyers should never ask to use their own shipping account to ship an item. They will pay you to ship the item. Beware of any buyer who wants you to use their FedEx or UPS shipping account for an eBay purchase.

ADVANCED SHIPPING SCAM

A scam seller posts an auction for an expensive item. A buyer wins the auction. The scammer puts off the buyer saying they will have to calculate shipping or they will send an invoice the next day or two. The scam seller uses a stolen credit card and has the item drop shipped from a legitimate company like Amazon.com to the buyer before receiving payment. The seller says they want payment by Western Union and they have already shipped the item. They then claim the bidder can wait until they receive the item to send payment just to show the seller is legitimate. The buyer receives the item and thinks everything is OK so they send the payment. The scam seller can threaten to call the police if the buyer does not send payment. The credit card owner sees the unauthorized charge and files a chargeback. The company may write off the loss or they may contact the police because they have the shipping address the item was shipped to. The police show up and now the auction buyer is in trouble and the scam seller has already received his payment and disappeared.

"NOT A SCAM" SCAM

My mystery envelope is not a scam

Any auction that has to say "*My auction is not a scam*" is a scam.

Beware of auctions that claim they are "legitimate", "100% genuine", "I'm Verified", "Not a Scam" Or "You can trust me, check my feedback" These tip-off phrases frequently mean the scammer has setup several accounts and used them to leave fake feedback for his account which proclaims himself as a great and honest seller.

Be careful of any seller who has to state in their auction that they are in compliance with eBay rules. This usually means they are on the edge of breaking eBay rules and walking a fine line.

CURRENCY EXCHANGE SCAM

Some criminal sellers on eBay offer eBooks that have land or currency information claiming the land or currency is about to be very valuable. They then recommend a website where you can purchase these items which is, of course, run by the person who sold the eBook. If someone knows inside information that is reliable, they will use it themselves and not sell it on eBay for one cent.

THIRD PARTY RECOMMENDATIONS

Beware of any email that claims to vouch for the legitimacy or honesty of ANYONE. If you are involved in an eBay transaction and receive an email from any sender that claims '*the seller is in good standing and is trustworthy to do business with*' then you are dealing with a scammer. These emails appear to come from eBay, PayPal, SquareTrade, or another company, or even a fake website the scammer setup. No company will vouch for the legitimacy of anyone on the Internet other than themselves. All of these emails are fakes sent by scammers.

CREDIT CARD CHARGE BACKS

Some sellers have their own merchant accounts and can accept credit cards. There are also services that allow sellers to offer products and the company charges the credit card for the seller. PayPal can also charge a credit card and deposit the money into the seller's PayPal account.

A chargeback occurs when the owner of the credit card contests the charge. The owner calls their credit card company and claims they did not make the purchase.

A chargeback can occur for a number of reasons. Some legitimate reasons are:
- The card number was stolen by a scammer.
- The card owner does not recognize the charge from XYZ Company
- The card owner's spouse made the charge without telling him/her.
- The card owner forgot about the purchase.

Some non-legitimate reasons are:

- The card owner did not receive the item or was dissatisfied, but was not honest enough to contact the seller about the matter.
- The card owner is short of cash and decides to recover some money they have spent, but they also want to keep the items they bought.
- The card owner has buyer's remorse and wants their money back, but they also want to keep the item for free.
- The card owner planned the scam from the start and intended to file a chargeback.

Sometimes the cardholder will wait an excessively long time before filing a chargeback. Scammers know this will more frequently result in a successful chargeback. Credit companys will allow someone to file a chargeback 90 days or more after the charge. After 90 days, the tracking information is no longer available as proof the item was shipped. Scammers know this and they will try to take advantage of this fact by waiting to file a fraudulent chargeback.

Normal people review credit card statements within a week of receiving them. If there is a problem, they will either contact the company making the charge or file a chargeback. Normal people do not wait 90 days or more before filing a chargeback.

PayPal's policy is designed to protect PayPal. If a buyer files a chargeback on a payment that was made using a credit card through PayPal, then PayPal will take the money out of the seller's account. If the seller cannot prove delivery, he may lose the money.

This scam is usually perpetrated by small time criminals and people who are basically dishonest. The credit card company will not allow someone to file an excessive number of chargebacks so they can only do this once in a while.

EARLY AUCTION ENDINGS

When a seller ends an auction early to 'sell to the high bidder', it usually means the high bidder and seller made a back door deal to sell at a higher price off of eBay. This saves the seller eBay fees. Sellers have no reason to end an auction early unless they have a deal for a lot more money. Why end an auction early when more bidders may bid higher? Honest sellers never end auctions early to 'sell to the current high bidder'.

Some sellers offer Gift Cards. These are specialty cards that are purchased with a cash value to be used at a specific store. You commonly see these at retailer's checkout areas; $20 Wal-Mart Gift Card. These are activated when they are paid for at the cashier.

This is a scam that can target both buyers and sellers. As a buyer, you have no sure way of knowing if the card has been activated. The cards could be stolen and therefore useless because they were never activated. The cards also could have been used or partially used. That $100 gift card you bought for $20 may only have $1 left on it. The card that is good at the auction close, may have no value when it reaches you because the seller used it just before shipping the card.

Gift cards are subject to fees. If a $20 gift card is purchased and not used for a year, it may be subject to a $2/month fee which makes it worthless now. All of it's value has evaporated in fees. Beware of anyone trying to sell a gift card they purchased last Christmas.

As a seller, you may have scammers contact you and ask for a scan of the card to verify it is real or that you have it. They may also ask for the number on the back and the security code(not all cards use security codes some just use the number on the back) so they can verify it is legitimate and check the balance at the store's website. These are tricks to obtain the number. Once the scammer has the number, they can use the number to make online purchases. They do not need the physical card. Now the seller will sell the card to the high bidder, but the value has already been spent by the scammer. The buyer thinks they have been scammed and the seller thinks the buyer is falsely claiming the card is no good so the seller thinks they are being scammed by the buyer. The scammer who never intended to purchase the card actually scammed them both.

Most gift cards have a toll-free number on the back to verify the amount on the card. No one needs the security code to check the balance. A buyer cannot be certain the number they were given by the seller is the number that will be on the card they will receive. A seller may have one good card and twenty worthless cards. They would only give the number from the good card to anyone wanting to verify it using the toll free number.

EBay limits the number of gift cards a seller can list within a time frame. This can slow down a scamer, but a good scammer has several scams going at once. Sellers may also resort to Leet Speak to list G1ft cards instead of Gift cards to continue listing worthless cards.

Beware of any seller offering a number of the same cards. The seller may have shop-lifted the cards all at once or they may not plan to ship anything.

Beware of anyone who repeatedly emails you regarding the value of the card. These people are attempting some type of scam and will usually request the card number and security code. Legitimate buyers will not be irrationally interested in the value. They will bid or they will not, based on your feedback and auction. An honest buyer may ask how they can verify the card is good. Anyone who demands verification is a scammer.

Always beware of anyone who is too interested in an item, anyone who tries to create a sense of urgency, or anyone who tries to put you on the defensive.

Scammers may also purchase gift cards using stolen credit cards or hijacked PayPal accounts. They are glad to pay more than the value because they are exchanging bad money for good. This is not common because experienced scammers are more interested in cash and not in using a gift card to buy stuff. Scammers would be more likely to post a similar auction without shipping anything. Inexperienced scammers or teenage crooks may purchase gift cards for more than their value using hijacked PayPal accounts. They would be interested in actually using the card to buy items for themselves and their friends.

In this auction an experienced buyer paid $54.01 for a gift card worth $50. The second high bidder bid $53.50, and other bids were $52, $50.99 and $50. I guess some people enjoy scamming themselves.

REFURBISHED

This is not exactly a scam, but many buyers feel they have been scammed from these auctions. If the seller sells a refurbished item and claims it is new or does not reveal it is refurbished, it could be considered a scam. Usually, bidders simply do not read the auction description thoroughly.

EBay is an excellent place to find refurbished or store returned items. When large chain stores receive a return, they send it to a liquidator to be sold for pennies on the dollar. These items can be a great bargain..or not. I have purchased many refurbished items and been very pleased with them. Other items have been a waste of money. When someone returns an item to a store, they return it for a reason. If someone returns a computer that shuts down after three hours and the liquidator tests it and sees that it boots up with no problems, the liquidator will sell it as a good item and even state it was tested. It was tested and it did work, but it still has a problem which is why it was returned in the first place.

Refurbished items are also favored offerings from scammers. Scammers can offer popular items at too-good-to-be-true pricing, and by saying Refurbished Like New, they can make it seem believable. When purchasing refurbished or store return merchandise, make sure you understand the risks you are taking when you bid.

DETAILED RETURN POLICIES

Any seller who has an extremely long and detailed return policy should be avoided.

There is something not-quite-right about sellers who feel the need to exonerate themselves from any responsibility in advance or who disclaims all liability if the buyer does not buy insurance. Lengthy policies usually indicate dishonest sellers. These are not career criminals. They are sellers who want to take advantage of other people and use their policy to do it. The seller is trying to escape responsibility for a bad transaction before the sale is even made.

RESHIPPER SCAM

A person sees a job advertisement for work-at home, or envelope stuffing, or some other at-home job. They respond and, surprise, surprise, they are accepted. The job seeker then gives all of their personal information including their social security number to this hiring company they have never heard of. They are then given instructions stating they will be re-shipping items from the US to the company in Romania or Nigeria or wherever. The company will explain that they are not allowed to establish a business presence in the US for legal reasons and need someone to ship to them as an individual.

Now, the company has a dupe willing to re-ship packages no questions asked. The scammer wins an auction and pays using a stolen credit card. The scammer has the package sent to the US address of their re-shipper. The seller never knows the buyer is in Nigeria. The payment is reversed because a stolen credit card was used and all of the sellers who were scammed now realize they have been scammed. They contact the police. The police visit the shipping address. The person at that address explains they were hired by a company in Nigeria to re-ship packages. The re-shipper now has a serious problem. When they took the job as a re-shipper, they provided all of their personal information to the scammer including their social security number. The scammer can now steal their identity, open new credit cards in their name using other accomplices and ruin the persons credit while stealing tens of thousands of dollars more.

Some people are recruited through chat rooms by people who befriend them. Some even convince the person in the US that they are boyfriend and girlfriend, then they offer them the 'opportunity' for this job. The scammer may claim to be in London or Australia and later reveal the company they work for has a branch in Nigeria looking for someone in the US to work for them.

These schemes usually last several weeks before they are exposed. Re-shipping or envelope stuffing are scams. No legitimate company will hire an individual to re-ship packages.

This scam is not limited to Nigeria. It could be for any country or even re-shipment within the US. This scam is not limited to eBay and the scammer may use stolen credit cards to purchase items from any online company. Re-shipper scams should be reported to the FBI Economic and Financial Crimes Commission.

MONEY ORDER

As a buyer:
When sending a money order always use delivery confirmation. If the seller says he did not receive the payment, you then have proof he did. If the seller claims he did not receive the money order on the day it was delivered, you can file immediately for a refund on the money order as lost or stolen. If this is done quickly enough, you may be able to recover your funds. Simply request delivery confirmation when sending your payment and write down the delivery confirmation number.

As a seller:
Money Orders are easily counterfeited. Scammers can purchase real money orders for low amounts. They re-print them for higher values. A seventy five cent money order can become a seventy five dollar money order or they may wash off the ink and completely reprint the face. Treat money orders just like checks. Wait until they clear before shipping.

KNOWN FRAUD CENTERS

Indonesia, Romania, Philippines, Russia, Ukraine

Indonesia is a well known fraud center. PayPal can disable a user's account for sending money to or receiving money from Indonesia. Romania is a well known source of fraudulent sales especially in the eBay Motors area. Criminals offer expensive items on eBay and request payment by Western Union be sent to Romania. No one who sends a Western Union payment to Romania or Indonesia ever receives the item. The Philippines, Russia and the Ukraine are also well known havens for criminals. You should refuse any order that requests shipment to these countries or any seller who requests payment be sent to any of these countries.

> *I once sold a book to someone in Argentina and shipped by Air Mail as the buyer requested. Global Priority mail with delivery confirmation is not available in Argentina because of their third world mail system. Two weeks later the buyer filed a PayPal complaint. I could not prove delivery because there is no delivery confirmation for Air Mail. This person did not contact me first or ask for the shipping status. They also filed the complaint at exactly the same time delivery was expected. I know they did receive the item; otherwise they would have waited longer or contacted me first. The buyer selected the least expensive shipping option knowing it did not offer delivery confirmation. This buyer committed fraud. If I had shipped by a more expensive carrier that offered tracking I could have proven delivery and avoided the PayPal reversal. I no longer ship to South or Central America without a tracking number because of instances like this and I never ship to Mexico for any reason.*

ROUND-ABOUT SCAM

This scam does not involve driving in a circle. It involves a large seller who offers lots of electronics.

The seller will post an item and claim it is 100% working and tested. When the buyer receives it and complains it is non-working, the seller offers to issue a refund for the returned item minus a 20% restocking fee. The buyer returns the bad merchandise and the seller issues the partial refund. The seller keeps the 20% restocking fee plus the handling costs. The seller then re-sells the same item again, over and over, round and round. The seller makes 20% of the item's cost plus any handling fees on every sale and they never have to replace inventory as long as the buyer returns the item. If the buyer does not bother to return the item, the seller keeps all of the money. This is also a common scam outside of eBay for computer parts. Beware of any seller who charges a high restocking fee.

A variation of this scam involves a repair center in collusion with the seller. The scam seller asks the buyer to send the item to a 'repair center'. Once sent to the repair center, the buyer is told the item is not repairable and they are charged for testing the item plus return shipping. The seller is the repair center at a different address. They sell store returns or known bad merchandise as good, then charge for a repair inspection that always results in the item being impossible to repair.

This type of scam is perpetrated by dishonest businesses. Excessive restocking fees are signs of fraudulent companies. If you find yourself in one of these scams, either file for a PayPal refund or a chargeback on your credit card as fast as possible.

Subscription Scams

There are many complaints about scam magazine subscriptions. The delivery window is 45-60 days which is outside of the eBay and PayPal complaint window. Many people do not receive their first issue for 3 to 5 months. This leads many to believe they have been scammed. Some do not receive their subscriptions, but most do.

There are many honest subscription sellers on eBay. These people receive a small payment or points for each person they sign up for the subscription. The magazine companies hope the subscriber will remain a subscriber and the subscriber will at least increase their circulation numbers which means they can charge more for advertising. Many of the subscriptions are bargain prices from 99 cents to a few dollars with free shipping. This is one exception to the 99 cent scam rule. The sellers obtain benefits other than the sale price in this case. It is unlikely a seller would bother to scam someone for under $10. Look for sellers who specialize in magazine subscriptions and offer a large variety. Check the feedback of the seller. Do not look for feedback from people who bought and are 'looking forward' to receiving something. Look for feedback from people who say 'The first issue came today'.

Magazine agents are not allowed to sell subscriptions on eBay. Their contract prohibits it. A few still do. Magazine subscription prices are strictly regulated by the publishers. Agents caught selling on eBay can have their magazine agent account suspended.

The major publishers do not allow their magazine subscriptions to be sold on eBay.

Keep it simple

Any transaction that seems complicated or confusing should be avoided. Transactions should be simple. Bid, win, pay by PayPal, receive the item within 2 weeks at most. Any seller or buyer who wants you to follow detailed instructions is trying to scam you.

I want to send a present to my sister but I do not want her to know it is from me. Put your name on the return address and I will paypal you extra $1000, include a cashiers check for $1000 in the box too and send by fedex overnight, I will pay for the extra shipping costs too, mark the package as a gift and the value as $20, and dont say anything to the police.

I'm turning you in to the FBI

What if a buyer threatens to turn you into the FBI, FTC, BBB, or any other agency they can think of? As long as you ran an honest auction and honored your posted policies as well as eBay rules and did not break the law, you should not have anything to worry about. The FBI receives thousands of crackpot calls every day. It is unlikely this person would even bother looking up the FBI's number, but if they did, so what? Who cares? The operator would quickly size them up as a nutcase. If they were successful in starting an investigation, you could probably sue them for filing a false police report.

Such threats are usually idle threats. If you have dealt in a fair and honest way with a seller and they have been unreasonable or demanding or make threats, you can be sure they are simply trying to defraud you. The buyer may use this same tactic with every seller they buy from to obtain a refund and keep the item purchased.

Private Feedback

EBay has an option for users to make their feedback private. Members can no longer sell if they make their feedback private. There is no legitimate reason for any member to make their feedback private. No matter what reason a seller claims, it is usually a lie. I have seen them all *"EBay made a mistake...."*, *"They are confusing me with this other guy I don't know and leaving neg feedback for me"*. They are all false. Some scammers claim they make feedback private to protect the identities of bidders, but if bidders wanted privacy, they would not leave feedback for the seller. A simple user search will show what the person's buying or selling history is so they are not hiding their transactions anyway.

Meet the seller
Seller: ebayscammer123 (Private)
Feedback: **50% Positive**

Members who hide their feedback have something to hide.

I'M REALLY REALLY REALLY INTERESTED

Beware of any buyer who is too interested in an item.

Scammers may send several messages about an item expressing great interest and trying to obtain a direct sale outside of eBay. They may use this method to create familiarity so the seller is more comfortable accepting a non standard form of payment when the party becomes high bidder. Sending a lot of emails, especially if they have lots of pointless details not related to the transaction, is a method scammers use to make the victim feel close to them and trust them.

Shared Feedback

Look at a sellers feedback profile and compare the users who left feedback. Were all of the accounts that left feedback created at about the same time? Do they all have roughly the same low feedback level? A seller with twenty feedback ratings from twenty different users that were created at the same time with twenty feedback ratings each is a sign of a scammer. The scammer created a number of accounts and used them to build fake feedback ratings for each other. The scammer will now use one as a seller account until it is disabled. Then they will use the next until it is disabled.

Personal PayPal

Personal PayPal accounts are for personal use and for sending auction payments. Not for accepting auction payments. Avoid any seller who insists payments by made from an existing PayPal balance. These sellers are trying to use a personal account for eBay purchases which is a violation of PayPal rules. Don't let them trick you into breaking any auction or PayPal rules. Payments to a Personal PayPal account also have less protection for the buyer and if they are used to pay for an auction, they may have no protection.

Also beware of anyone who wants to pay or receive payments below a certain amount or splits up payments instead of paying all at once. They are trying to stay under minimum transfer limits.

Beware of any seller who has bad grammar, spelling, or types in ALL CAPS. I am not talking about a simple *missspelling. I meen a serous mispealing.*

I NEVER BUY FROM ANYONE WHO POSTS AN AUCTION IN ALL CAPITAL LETTERS. The likelihood of problems with the transaction increases when you buy from someone who posts an auction in all capital letters. Posting an auction in all caps is not only a violation of Net Etiquette, but it is downright rude. All caps are considered SHOUTING on the Internet. No one wants to buy from someone who is shouting at them. When I first started using eBay, I would buy from sellers who used all caps. I quickly realized those auctions resulted in problems with the seller most of the time. Sometimes the seller did not described the item correctly, or they could not figure out how to cash a money order once they had it, or they packed the item poorly and it was broken, or they simply never bothered to ship the purchase. There is always a problem when dealing with an ALL CAPs seller.

I also ignore any feedback comments by anyone WHO POSTS RESPONSES IN ALL CAPITALS. They simply cannot be trusted to give an honest comment.

> *It is always inappropriate to post messages or auctions using all capital letters. That is SHOUTING and it is rude. ALL CAP auctions usually indicate an inexperienced person or a scammer trying to grab people's attention. Never buy from a seller who posts auctions in all CAPS.*

Description
THIS ITEM IN VERY GOOD CONDTION. I AM MOVING AND MY SAYS I MUST SELL IT. THEIR IS NO PLACE FOR IT IN THE NEW HOUSE. I SHIP BY THE FAST MEANS IF YOU BUY BEFORE IT IS GONE.

Would you trust this seller? There are a number of warning signs here.

> *There is a caveat to the ALL CAPS rule. Terminals for the blind sometimes use all capital letters. If a blind person has such a terminal, they should set it to use all lower case instead. No one knows if an all caps auction came from a blind terminal and will assume it was by an inexperienced, unprofessional or scammer seller.*

Sellers who post in all CAPS, or cannot spell, or do not use correct grammar are more likely to be problem sellers or outright fraudulent sellers.

These sellers are usually young children, non-English speaking scammers, or simply incompetent sellers.

Scammers who cannot speak English often use translation websites which produce choppy and nonsense English. Just because someone does this does not make it a scam.

The phrase "please send the money quickly" translated to German and back to English using one of these websites becomes "send please the money fast"

English: please send the money quickly
German: senden Sie bitte das Geld schnell
Back to English: send please the money fast

Anyone who emails with this type of language, is using a translator website.

There is a caveat to the poor grammar rule. Deaf people, those who cannot hear and became deaf before they learned to speak, frequently have bad grammar. English is a spoken language and there are many nuances that are learned from speaking it. Deaf people never learned English by speaking it. There may be many deaf people with excellent grammar, but there are very intelligent deaf people with very poor grammar. With experience you can usually spot a post by a deaf person. It is different than a post by someone who learned English as a second language or a child. When you see a bad grammar post, keep in mind that it could have been posted by a deaf person.

It's Worth $20 Zillion Dollars

Beware of sellers who quote extraordinarily high estimated prices in their auctions and especially in the titles. These sellers try to make a $200 item sound like it is worth $20,000 when in fact they are usually selling a counterfeit worth $10. This is common in categories where buyers may know that an item is valuable, but they are unfamiliar with actual pricing such as high end designer clothing and top of the line jewelry like Rolex Watches.

TX 4 UR NTREST

Auctions that use text messaging abbreviations are usually posted by children. Children use these abbreviations when talking to their friends on instant messengers or cellphone texting. They use the same language when they post auctions. An auction that is peppered with UR instead of YOUR or YOU'RE, N1 for Nice One, NE1 for Anyone, IOW for In Other Words is written by someone experienced with text messaging. Such abbreviations are appropriate in text messages, but not for auctions or other business communications. It is not unusual for someone to end with TFL(Thanks For Looking) but if the text is filled with needless abbreviations, this usually indicates the auction was posted by a child.

Positive Feedback Guaranteed

Never bid on an auction that promises positive feedback if the item is inexpensive. EBay will cancel the accounts of both buyers and sellers who they believe are buying or selling feedback. If an auction is for a one cent item with a buy-it-now price, this is quite obvious. If the auction is for an item that no one would want and it is being sold for $1, it may also be obvious. If the seller implies they are in no hurry for payment, this is pretty obvious and eBay can spot it as easily as you can. If you purchase a low priced auction, $5 or less, and the seller even mentions positive feedback in the auction, you may be putting your account in jeopardy.

It is best to avoid even the appearance of buying or selling feedback. Stay away from auctions that promise positive feedback if they are for inexpensive items.

Confirm By Phone

Always talk to the seller by phone when purchasing an expensive item($1000 or more) **before** sending payment.

Beware of sellers who appear to be in the US but cannot speak English well. Scammers with US phone numbers may be using VOIP phone service and actually be in another country. They may also be in the US just to run scam operations.

I Have A Customer

Beware of any buyer who says "*I have a customer who is interested in your item...*" This is always a scam. If a buyer has a customer they want to resell to, they will never tell you. They will simply buy the item. Statements like these always lead into a next-step. The scammer will try to gain the seller's confidence or will want to use their customer as an excuse for an unusual payment method.

Fill Out This File

Beware of any buyer or seller who sends you a file, any type of file, and asks you to fill it out to verify your legitimacy or to process a payment. These files are always trojan programs. Even PDF files should not be trusted because they may not really be PDF files. Legitimate sellers will never send you a file to 'fill-out'. They will accept payment by PayPal or if they take credit cards, they will send you a link to a secure SSL(https://) website.

These trojan programs will infect your computer and send all of your personal information, PayPal and eBay passwords, every keystroke you type, to the criminal. You should have both Anti-Virus and Firewall software on your computer to protect against such trojans.

Multiple Credit Cards

Beware of any buyer who wants to pay by credit card but sends more than one card number to you. Legitimate buyers will only provide one card number to a seller if they provide any. Normally they will use their card through an online gateway or through PayPal. Legitimate buyers will never send a credit card number by email and they absolutely will not send two or more.

Multiple Checks

Beware of any buyer who sends multiple Cashier's Checks. If a buyer purchases an expensive item, then sends three cashiers checks totaling more than the value of the item, it is a scam every time. If a purchaser sends a money order that is limited to $150 plus a second for $25 totaling the item price of $175, that is understandable. If the buyer purchases an item for $1000 and sends three cashiers checks for $1000 each, that is a scam. The buyer will ask for a 'refund' and they will claim they have an emergency. They will ask that the overpayment minus a *fee-for-your-trouble* be wired back to them. The checks are counterfeit. Once the money is sent to the scammer the bank returns the counterfeit checks and cancels the credit to the depositor's bank account.

Suspect Listings

If you are suspicious about a listing, look for similar listings elsewhere. Search for the exact title or exact text from an auction in previous closed auction listings and also search Google. Scammers often steal ads from classified ad sites or re-use the same scam ad over and over. You may find the exact phrase, *"it be a great boat with 255 Horse, Excusrion Model"* appeared in ten online classified ads posted by ten different people.

Car History Tricks

Carfax reports are not the whole story. These are only a small piece of information and may not reveal important defects or the true vehicle history. If a seller gives a VIN stolen from another auction listing, then the CarFax information is meaningless. Cars can be totaled or salvaged without ever having those designations added to the title. If an owner sells a vehicle directly to a restoration shop or to a salvage yard that re-sells the papers and VIN to organized crime, then the buyer has no way of knowing the real history of the vehicle. Vehicles are also illegally transferred by middlemen. One person buys the car but never registers it. They then give the paperwork to someone else or they sell it to a third person and fill out the paperwork as if the original owner made the sale to the third person. This is called Jumping and it is illegal. Jumping sales will not appear in CarFax reports. The owner hands the paperwork to a middleman, the middleman does not fill out anything but then gives the title to a restoration shop. The restoration shop pieces two wrecked vehicles together and then sells the result to a new owner without ever registering the vehicle themselves, without ever revealing it was totaled, and without telling the buyer.

A dishonest repair shop may take a VIN and/or the speedometer/computer from a new totaled vehicle and put it on a high mileage used car to be re-sold as a low mileage vehicle. The end buyer does not know the real history.

Beware of any seller offering an expensive vehicle who does not want the buyer to have a mechanic look at the vehicle before payment is made. Always have a vehicle inspected before paying for it.

Police Car Scams

Used police cars and government surplus vehicles are common scams on and off of eBay. These vehicles are in much worse condition than indicated or the seller may not even have them. Less than honest sellers as well as outright scammers frequently inflate horsepower or gas mileage numbers. Many people expect ex-police cars to have high horsepower. They may actually be cheap models that are low horsepower, but the seller will claim they are high horsepower models. The average person does not know the real horsepower ratings of police model vehicles. Police use vehicles heavily and they stay in service as long as possible. These vehicles, if the seller actually has a vehicle, are severely worn out by the time they are sold. Use common sense and inspect before paying.

Homemade Item Scams

Beware of homemade items like cleaning solutions, make-up, and skin care products. You have no idea what these really contain and there is something mentally off-kilter about anyone who mixes up their own car-soap solution to sell on eBay.

These products may have no labels or labels printed out on the person's home printer. If it were really good, they would produce the product in quantity and market it to major stores. There are legitimate homemade products on eBay, but some products simply should not be purchased as homemade items. If someone offers an item with a brand name, but you cannot find any information on the Internet, and you cannot find a website for the product, it should be avoided.

Some of these homemade solutions include home-fabricated electronics such as vehicle upgrade chips or gas-saving devices. These may be nothing more than an empty box with connectors on them. They may contain useless circuits or even cause damage to your vehicle.

Other homemade devices may include 'power pyramids' someone soldered together, kits for perpetual motion machines, levitation devices, and flying machines. These are almost always scams. If the devices really worked or were practical to build, the person would be building the device and not selling a homemade kit or plans.

I'm a __(Insert Authority Figure Here)__

Beware of sellers who claim affiliation that will make them seem more trustworthy. If a seller claims they are a member of law enforcement, the fire department, a charity, the government, or any other organization that could make them seem more legitimate, they are less legitimate. Anyone can make these claims. Only those who feel a need to gain the trust of other people will actually state these claims in their auctions. A legitimate seller may offer an old fireman's coat and state they are a volunteer fireman. A non-legitimate seller will sell a 4-Wheeler and make a point of stating they are a police officer with some specific city and they have served for ten years. This second example is trying to gain the buyer's trust with their claims. Beware of any seller or buyer who tries too hard to gain trust.

I've Been In Business 30 Years

Beware of sellers who claim they have been in business a long time without real proof. If their eBay ID says they registered a month ago and they claim they have been in business 30 years, they are trying to gain buyer's trust. Anyone claiming they have been in business five, ten, twenty, or more years would have registered on eBay years ago, not a month ago. This seller is trying to gain buyer's trust too hard.

Sales Tax

It is illegal to charge sales tax on auction sales if you do not have a state sales tax number. Beware of any seller who charges sales tax if you are not in the same state. That is always a scam because sales tax can only be charged in the state where the seller runs his business.

SHADY SELLER CHECK

Before buying from any seller we must ask some basic questions. There is no reason to look further into the auction or the value of the item if the seller cannot be trusted. The majority of scams are possible because buyers either do not look at the seller's feedback at all or do not look deeply enough.

Looking at the seller's feedback percentage is not enough. Many bidders mistakenly think the feedback percentage indicates the trustworthiness of the seller. The feedback percentage can be misleading. A highly rated seller with 100% positive feedback and 1000 transactions may look very trustworthy, but what if the account has been taken over by a criminal? You may not be buying from the person you thought you were.

The seller's feedback is the starting point. It is not unusual to have some negative comments, but sellers should not have too many. How many negatives have they received in the last month versus the number of sales they have made? The last 12 months? If the seller has a long history of positive feedback and suddenly they have 4 or 5 recent negatives, that may indicate the account has been hijacked by a criminal. A recent string of negative comments from different people is a bad sign.

What do the negative comments say? Are the people posting negative comments believable or just bad apples themselves? What is the feedback rating of those leaving negative feedback? Just because a seller has a bad feedback rating or several over time does not mean the seller is dishonest or unreliable. Feedback comments from low rated members that say "*bad seller*" or "*where is my stuff*" can be ignored. Comments like these do not contain any details about the transaction. These terse comments usually indicate problem buyers. Comments like "*two weeks and no product, seller will not respond to email*" are much more informative. If a seller has a number of such comments, be careful about dealing with them.

Are those leaving the seller negative feedback themselves trustworthy? Look at their feedback ratings. Feedback can tell a lot about a seller or buyer. Do they have other negatives from sellers? Do they have a history of leaving negative feedback? Normally, eBay buyers should rarely need to leave negative feedback. Any buyer who makes a habit of leaving negative feedback should not be trusted.

If the seller has 100 or fewer feedback ratings, compare the people who have left feedback for the seller with those leaving feedback for these people. Are the same members who left this seller feedback also leaving feedback for everyone who has left feedback for this seller? That is unusual and it looks like one person has created 100 or more accounts and is sharing feedback among them to build up feedback ratings.

Are a large number of the people who left feedback for the seller No Longer Registered Users? This may indicate the accounts are all connected and a number of them have already been exposed as scammers and disabled.

The seller's own words can often reveal the scam.

When you are reading over the description, pay attention to what is listed and especially what is not listed. Is the seller offering a vintage radio without saying if it works or not? Is the seller explaining the rare mark on the bottom of a vase, but fails to show a photograph of it? Is the seller offering an expensive item with no photos or only blurry photos? It can be obvious if the seller is hiding something. Even if they are not intentionally hiding something, you can quickly figure out whether or not you want to do business with them. Dishonest or inexperienced, either way, sellers who hide important information are sellers to avoid.

Does the seller have a Reserve Price? Sellers with reserve prices are usually inexperienced. Even if they have large feedback ratings they are inexperienced. Selling a lot of items does not necessarily make someone an experienced seller. They may be losing money on every auction and not even realize it. Scammers may use reserve prices in illogical ways. They may set a reserve price that is higher than the value of the item, then say what the reserve price is in the auction while offering a Buy-It-Now option at a lower price. This pressures viewers to use the Buy-It-Now price. Bidders want to receive a bargain and may even think they are taking advantage of the seller if the Buy-It-Now price is far below the value of the item.

Is there an unusual urgency in the auction? Scam artists often try to trick bidders into contacting them directly by using an urgent plea. They may claim they are moving out of the country, they are in a divorce, or they need surgery. They may have a Buy-It-Now price that sounds too good to be true or run a one day auction. All of these are warning signs that this seller should not be trusted.

Does the seller request, or even demand, that bidders contact them before bidding. This is a common scam. The dishonest sellers will offer the item at a bargain price to everyone who calls. They then take the money and disappear.

Does the seller make negative statements or threats in the listing? If the seller spoke to you in the tone of their auction, would you want to do business with them? Avoid sellers with bad attitudes or an axe to grind.

Does the seller list shipping costs? Beware of sellers who either do not state shipping costs or who list excessively high shipping.

Does the seller say in the description or in the payment options they accept PayPal? There is something not quite right about a regular seller who does not accept PayPal. Why can they not obtain a PayPal account? Not having a PayPal account makes sending a payment more difficult and less reliable. Sellers who accept PayPal are always preferred over those who do not.

Where is the seller located? Is it local, is it in another country, do they hide where they are located? Never trust a seller who does not want anyone to know the country they are shipping from. The location is shown at the top of the auction. Beware of sellers who show USA as their location, but clearly do not speak English. These are frequently scammers in other countries who pretend to be in the USA.

Does the seller require or prefer an unusual payment method? Any seller who requests Western Union payments should not be trusted. Offering Western Union as an option is acceptable, but insisting on it is completely unacceptable. Any seller asking for unusual payment methods or to use any payment website not on eBay's approved payment services list should be avoided.

Any seller who wants to use an escrow service other than escrow.com should be reported to eBay security. Escrow fraud is very common. Do not trust any member who wants to use a different escrow company.

Is it too good to be true? Why is this seller $200 cheaper than anyone else? Is it worth $200 to risk being ripped off for $500? It is better to pay a few dollars more and buy from a seller with a longer history and good feedback than it is to risk buying from a seller with no feedback history. Scammers make offers that are too good to be true.

Never buy from anyone with a zero feedback rating or only feedback for low priced buys. Scammers often setup a new account and either begin selling immediately or make some token purchases for 99 cent items to build their feedback.

Never buy from a new member who has a lot of icons by their name or in their auction meant to imply trust or endorsement. New members may use ID Verify, but no legitimate member will use ID Verify and join Square Trade and be a Power Seller. This person is trying too hard to gain people's trust.

Beware of any Power Seller with under 100 feedback. Power Sellers should sell lots of items or expensive items. If you see a Power Seller who has very low feedback, look at their selling history. Does it make sense? They may be legitimate, but it is unusual for a low rated member to be a Power Seller.

In the seller's feedback section click on 'Feedback Left For Others' to see what feedback the seller has left. Do the comments sound intelligent or like they were made by a child? Does the seller leave any feedback for others? If they do not leave feedback then do you want to buy from a discourteous seller who does not respond to positive feedback from others?

Has the seller previously been a buyer and seller of collector stamps, but now they have three auctions for three identical cars? It is very unusual for a stamp collector to suddenly jump into the car business. This looks like a hijacked account.

Click on some of the sellers past auctions. Compare the description and terms. Are the old auctions clearly different from the current auction? Did the seller previously use good grammar and spelling, but their new auctions contain bad grammar or are in all CAPS? Has the seller been using plain auctions and now they are using lots of graphics? This is a clear sign that the account owner is not the person who posted the current auctions.

Has the seller's terms suddenly changed from past auctions? If the seller always accepted PayPal and never offered Western Union, but the new auctions do not accept PayPal and do offer Western Union, this may not be the account owner's auction. It may also indicate that the account owner had their PayPal account cancelled for fraud.

Does the seller list an email address in the auction and insist any contact is done through this email and not through eBay's Message Center? Scammers often do not change email contact information because the account holder will receive a notification that it has been changed. Scammers can change other email preferences, such as notification when an auction is listed or ends without alerting the real account owner. If they change the primary contact email address, the account owner will be notified. Scammers do not want bidders to use the Message Center because those messages can go to the real account owner. Scammers often demand bidders contact them through an email address directly.

When was the seller's account created? It is **not** normal for someone to setup an account and start selling immediately. Never buy from anyone who has not been a member of eBay for at least 3 months. Scammers often create accounts, build feedback in a short period and then begin running auctions to scam buyers.

I'd rather give up the chance to win a low priced item than be ripped off by someone who I should have known was a scammer.

Check the eBay community message boards under the Community link at the top of every page. Search for the user's name in the messages. Many members may complain here instead of posting negative feedback.

It can be very difficult to find negative feedback for some sellers. Active sellers may receive hundreds of positive feedbacks a week. This buries the negative feedbacks. Generally this is a good sign. If it is hard to find negatives among the positives, then this seller appears to be doing a good job.

After checking all of these points we have to ask if we trust this seller. If we do not, then find another auction. If we do trust the seller, we can continue.

Avoid Becoming a Victim

- Never reply to email or pop-up messages asking for personal or financial information.
- Never click on links in email messages.
- Never copy and paste a link from the message into your Web browser. The link you see is not always the true destination link.
- Some scammers send emails that appear to be from a legitimate companies and ask you to update your information or claim there is a problem, or ask you to call a phone number to update your account. Never click on a link in one of these emails. Type the link in your browser if you want to login to your real account. Call the customer service telephone number for the company but NOT the number in the email. You can find the real number on your bank statement, on the real website, or in the phone book.
- Do use anti-virus and anti-spyware software, as well as a firewall, and update them all regularly. Use MyLittleMole.com toolbar and anti-virus software with a firewall.
- Never email personal or financial information to anyone. Never share your PayPal or eBay passwords with family or friends.
- Do review credit card and bank statements when you receive them to check for unauthorized charges and monitor them online. A $10 unauthorized charge may be a scammer's test to see if your card is good. Report any unauthorized charges.
- Never open any email attachment. These can contain viruses that will monitor your computer and send your eBay or PayPal information or other financial information to scammers. The person the email appears to be from may not be who really sent it.

PROTECT YOURSELF

HOW DO I PROTECT MYSELF?

Be aware of the most common scams we have covered. They will be easy to recognize and avoid now. Always check out a seller before bidding. Never share personal information with strangers. Beware of anyone who wants you to do anything unusual whether it is a strange shipping or payment request, or joining a website payment service, or using an unfamiliar escrow company. Beware of unusual requests. Never pay a seller using Western Union or MoneyGram.

Above all, if it sounds too good to be true, IT IS A SCAM.

You can also protect yourself by using antivirus programs. The software you use should offer a firewall which will alert you if a program tries to access the Internet without your permission, check email for viruses and Trojan programs which can monitor your computer keystrokes to steal passwords and worse.

The MyLittleMole.com toolbar will warn you or anyone in your household who forgets and clicks a link in a phishing email which leads to a look-alike eBay or PayPal website.

Always make sure you are on the real eBay or PayPal websites before typing your password.

CANCELING PAYPAL COMPLAINTS

Never cancel a PayPal complaint if the matter is not resolved. Some dishonest sellers will respond to PayPal complaints by emailing the buyer and apologizing for the problem, then they promise to ship the next day.

> *I am so sorry for the delay, my wife has been sick and I have been at the hospital. I just came home and found this complaint. I am again very sorry. I need to access my paypal account to pay some immediate bills but due to the complaint it is locked. I assure you that I will ship first thing in the morning if you can just cancel the complaint so I can access my funds for this emergency I would be greatful.*

The seller's account is not disabled because of the complaint. This is a trick. The seller wants the buyer to cancel the complaint because once a complaint is cancelled, it cannot be re-instated.

EBay has so many legitimate auctions, they can have difficulty finding the bad ones. They depend on members to report auctions that violate eBay rules. If you see an auction that violates eBay rules, you can easily report them. Reporting these auctions protects inexperienced buyers from falling for dishonest seller scams.

The *'Report This Item'* link is at the bottom of every auction listing or in the auction header information(depending on which view options you have selected). You simply fill out the eBay form with the offence and the item number. An eBay employee will check the auction for policy violations. Click the Email Support link at the end of the report to submit your final report to eBay. Reporting scammers prevents them from victimizing other, less informed members.

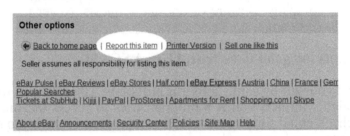

How do I keep my password secure?

There is nothing mysterious about a hijacker obtaining your password. The only place a hijacker can obtain your password is from you. You may type it into a look-alike site, you may install a Trojan program on your computer that grabs the password, or you may share your password with family or friends who in turn give it to a hijacker willingly or foolishly.

It's simple, don't cooperate with them. When a scammer sends an email with a link to a look-alike site, don't type your password. Make sure you are on the real site first.
Use anti-virus software. The anti-virus software that came with your computer is not adequate. These programs expire after a period and must be renewed or you must subscribe to their service to keep them working correctly. Anti-virus alone is not enough. You need a full protection suite like Zone Alarm that will alert you if a program tries to access the Internet and distribute your password or if you download a known virus or Trojan that could steal your password or monitor your keystrokes.

Remember, your passwords are for you and you alone. No one has any legitimate reason to ask you for your password. Not by email, not by phone, not in person. No friend or family member has any reason to even ask for your passwords either.

Cookies

When you access eBay or PayPal it creates a cookie that your browser uses to communicate with eBay. It tells eBay who you are. Make sure you remove all cookies from your computer if you sell or give it away. The option to remove cookies is under your browser security settings or privacy settings.

PAYPAL SECURITY KEY

For those really paranoid about their PayPal accounts, there is a secret key device that can help keep your account secure. PayPal offers a service which provides a special key fob that shows your current PayPal password. This password changes every time you login to your PayPal account. If a criminal does obtain your password, they cannot use it. The password will be different every time it is used. This key fob costs $5 and there is no monthly fee. You can find information on the key in the Security & Resolution Center
http://pages.ebay.com/securitycenter/security_key.html
Using a security key will prevent you from placing Snipe Bids. You can use a second buyer-only account for snipe bidding.

The PayPal security key changes your PayPal password constantly to prevent hackers from gaining access to your account.

CANCELING BIDS

If you are a seller and you see a suspect bidder, cancel the bid.

Check the feedback the bidders have left for others. If they have a habit of leaving negative feedback, cancel their bid and add them to your blocked bidders list. An honest buyer may leave an occasional negative, but he should not have a clear history of leaving negative feedback. If he has already won it is too late. Let the transaction go through and maybe you will not have a problem. Add the bidder to your blocked list anyway.

What do you do if you see a bidder on one of your auctions who has a history of non payment in their feedback? If the auction is in progress you can cancel their bid, add them to your blocked bidder list, and make sure the auction was setup to not allow anyone with less than five feedbacks to bid. This prevents the dishonest bidder from setting up a new account and immediately re-bidding under a new identity.

If the auction ended and this person sniped it or you simply did not notice their bid, don't do anything. Wait and see if the buyer pays. If they do not pay in 10 days, file the non payment notice. There is no reason to contact them and ask for payment. This is a person with a history of scamming sellers. If they still do not pay, then file for your final value credit. You may see their account immediately disabled if you are the third seller to file.

You should also cancel bids if you see a bidder with a high number of mutual feedback withdrawals. It is not unusual to have one or two over a career. It is unusual for a buyer to have several. Either this bidder picks nothing but crooked sellers or this is a problem bidder who receives bad feedback and then posts retaliatory feedback. If the buyer has a low overall feedback score, like 50, and eight withdrawals, this is a problem bidder. Remember to add this person to your blocked bidder list too.

Never let family or friends use your computer to access their PayPal or eBay accounts. You should not use their computers to access your account either. They may have a virus or Trojan on their computer that captures your login information and sends it to a criminal. Both eBay and PayPal keep track of where their users login from. If your friend does something to violate eBay or PayPal rules, eBay or PayPal may see your login from their computer and assume both accounts are controlled by the same person or your password has been compromised. This can cause your account to be disabled as well as theirs.

Never login to your PayPal or eBay account using a public terminal like a pay for access, Internet cafe, or a Wi-Fi system. You never know who is running these or who is monitoring them.

Your PayPal account can be disabled if a buyer pays using a stolen credit card. Some PayPal users think this is unfair. It is actually the smart move. PayPal has no way to determine if the person who made the stolen credit card payment was or was not the same person who is in control of the PayPal account the money was sent to. A criminal can steal a credit card number, use it to send a payment to a hijacked PayPal account, then transfer the money out of PayPal or purchase items using PayPal that they can resell locally. Freezing the PayPal account is necessary to stop the fraud if the account has been hijacked.

Never let other people use your computer to access their eBay or PayPal accounts.

Logging in to PayPal or eBay from a foreign country can cause your account to be immediately frozen. If PayPal sees someone login to your account from an Internet address outside of the USA when you are registered with a US address, it immediately raises a red flag. To eBay or PayPal this looks like your account has been compromised. Do not login to your PayPal account or eBay when you are vacationing outside the USA.

If you have a Paypal debit card, it will be deactivated if you use it outside of the USA(assuming you are registered in the USA). If you will be traveling, notify Paypal

You are having dinner with your neighbors and your neighbor's son asks to check his eBay account on your computer. He logs in and eBay sees he has logged in from a computer that is different from the one he usually uses. He then checks his PayPal balance too and logs out. He has an auction running offering an item that is against eBay rules. The auction closes with Buy-It-Now and someone sends payment before eBay can cancel the auction. EBay checks the auction after it is closed. PayPal receives a credit card payment using a stolen credit card number for the auction. They check to see what other accounts this person may have access to. In other words, what other accounts have logged in from a computer his account has used. They see that he logged in from your home computer. Now they disable his PayPal account and yours, and eBay disables your eBay accounts along wit his because this is not his first offence. EBay and PayPal have no way of knowing who is using your account, but they know for certain someone with access to your computer posted an illegal auction. PayPal has no way of knowing who was at the keyboard, but they know someone with an illegal auction accepted funds from a stolen credit card and this person used the same computer you use to login.

through the message center immediately before your trip so they can mark your card as OK for use outside the USA. This lasts about 2 weeks and must be done just before your trip because it cannot be scheduled.

> *If you suspect someone's account has been hijacked(taken over by a criminal), you can contact eBay. If they are slow to respond, you can place a bid and then request the personal information to obtain a phone number. Then call the seller and ask him if he is actually offering the item that has drawn your suspicion. Maybe the person has been buying and selling bisque figurines for months and now he is suddenly selling expensive professional audio equipment. No seller should object to a personal contact information request under these circumstances. You can place a minimum bid, request their information, then cancel the bid if the seller is not legitimate.*
>
> *If the seller insists on contact through email, use the Ask Seller A Question link. This may reach the real account owner if the hijacker has not changed the email address associated with the account.*

MY LITTLE MOLE TOOLBAR

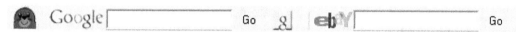

If you are on the Internet then you MUST have this FREE toolbar installed. Not only is it handy, it can protect you from fraud!

The My Little Mole^{TM} Tool Bar is a program that adds an additional toolbar to your Internet browser. It has some fancy searches that allow you to quickly search Google, eBay, and Amazon. These search features are very handy, but that is not what makes it so important.

The toolbar also compares websites you visit to known fraudulent websites. This includes fake PayPal and eBay look-alike sites. If you receive an email claiming you must update your PayPal information, or your bank information or any other fake message, and you click on the link without thinking, My Little Mole will warn you that the website is not the real PayPal, eBay, or other website.

If you have friends or family who may click links without thinking, you should make sure they install this toolbar. If it only catches one fraudulent website, you can save them many headaches as well as money.

You can download a free copy of My Little Mole^{TM} at http://www.MyLittleMole.com

The MyLittleMole. com toolbar shows a warning when a look-alike eBay webpage created by a scammer is loaded.

How do you stop a scammer. How do you get back at them when they are in another country?

I am NOT advising any of the following actions.

The below methods have been proposed by others and I am only relisting them here. The best option when you see a scam in progress is to report it to the proper authorities which may be PayPal, or eBay, or the police. I cover these to show how dangerous they are and try to explain why you should not do them.

Most scammers depend on those who recognize their scam to simply go away and ignore them. Those who do not recognize the scam continue communicating and the scammer can expect a big payoff from them. If everyone wasted the scammer's time then they would have less incentive and less time to scam others. At least this is the rationale behind some of the following methods.

Phishing Poison

Phishing poision means poisoning a scammers database by filling it with fake information. More simply, it means entering fake login names and passwords into their look-alike websites.

This works for both spammers and look-alike eBay or PayPal sites. These sites request a password for eBay or PayPal, but they have no way to authenticate the passwords. They do not know which are real and which are fake. When visiting one of these scam sites, you can enter any fake user ID/password combination and it will be accepted. You can continue to select fake options and enter fake information.

The scammers depend on people who recognize the fake site to click the back button and do nothing. This leaves the victims who do not realize it is fake to enter their information. Now the scammer has a nice summary of eBay or PayPal logins and passwords. If everyone who received the phishing email went to the site and logged in using several made up logins and passwords, the scammers database would be poisioned. One thousand emails would not result in ten PayPal accounts, it would result in thousands of fake logins and passwords. The scammer would have to test every one to find which was real and which was fake. This same technique works with spammers. Spammers setup fake websites that ask for credit card numbers. These sites do not use real time payment systems because they are fake sites. The credit card number is sent to the scammer and the victim sees a message saying their payment will be processed later. The scammer will then make thousands of dollars in unauthorized charges to the card. If everyone who received spam went to the spammer's site and entered fake credit card numbers, they would be accepted. The spammer has no real-time processing system and can only check the basic format of the card numbers. By entering fake credit card numbers and fake expiration dates, the site visitors have poisoned the spammers database. They now have thousands of bad card numbers they have to go through to find the few real numbers from victims. Poisoning scammer's or spammer's databases is fairly safe now, but the scammers could put malicious code in their sites that runs if, for example, they do not detect a card number of the correct number of digits. Some spammers already resort to using image verification to prevent their databases from being poisoned by automated scripts.

116

Email Floods

A scammer has an efficient business if they send a fake email to 1000 people and find ten victims. What if they suddenly had 1000 people emailing them ten times each, pretending to be interested in their scam? Now they have to sort through ten thousand emails to find the ten that are real. Flooding someone's email box with mail can be considered an attack which could be illegal. Sending ten messages in response to someone's message expressing an interest in their proposal, is hard to consider an attack. Especially when they appear to be sending the message only to you and you 'really' want to make sure your response is not lost.

This is a dangerous thing to do. The scammer can track the email address used or IP address. It may be obvious if you respond and use the same email the scammer mailed in the first place. The scammer can also Google for your email to find other information on you like your personal webpage or web postings which include personal information they could use against you.

eBay Vigilante

Setup a special eBay account and use it to bid outrageously high amounts on obvious fraudulent auctions. Then report the auction to eBay. This prevents anyone from winning the auction and being scammed. As the high bidder, you do not have to pay if the auction is cancelled, not even if it is nullified after the close time. If the auction is not cancelled, leave negative feedback warning others.

This is dangerous. For one, placing bids with no intent to pay is a violation of eBay rules. You may find not only this account, but your main account disabled for shill bidding. If you provide false registration information to prevent the scammer from knowing who you are, you have again violated eBay rules. If you are mistaken and the account has not been hijacked, you have now committed a criminal offence and could be explaining it to the FBI or be sued by the account owner.

Western Union Scammer

If a scam seller wants to receive payment by Western Union or other means, string them along. Do not reveal any personal information and if they ask, give fake information. Tell them the payment was sent to a specific Western Union office 90 miles from the one they wanted it to go to. The scammer will waste hours driving there and back only to receive nothing. If they ask why you did not send it to the requested outlet, say you tried but Western Union required such a large amount to be sent to a premium office location. You can also swear it was sent and that you will check on it to continue stringing the scammer along.

This is dangerous. You are messing with dangerous people who are involved in organized crime. I should not have to tell you how this could end if they realize you are wasting their time and costing them lots of money they could be scamming from others.

The scammer may decide to come after someone who has made them drive 90 miles out of their way on a wild goose chase. If the scammer knows the eBay ID of the person, they can easily bid on an auction by that person and request the seller's mailing address for a money order. The seller will have no idea they are talking to the scammer and will gladly turn over their real name and real address.

Non-English Speakers

If the scammers clearly do not speak English well, you can mess with them using phrases and complex terms that are common in the English language, but not in other languages.

I will send the Western Union Payment today. Thank you and get stuffed.

Non English speakers generally understand basic subject-verb-object sentences well. They do not understand complex sentence structures. These also do not translate through translation websites well. You can use complex sentence structures and unusual words.

I would be astonishingly gratified should thou be sending the goods as with the wind and will procure pay in the form of a Union of Western as with celerity as practicable and viable as the schedule of the day allows. As tala vista baby.

This can backfire just like the other methods. You may be dealing with a member of organized crime who would eventually show one of your emails to someone in their organization who can speak English.

Be Stupid

Scammers like to victimize people who cannot recognize a scam. Feign interest and keep asking pointless question. Pretend you are completely stupid and continue wasting the scammers time.

I would be happy to send payment. Please tell me who has a Western Union and how much does it weigh? I do not know if I can ship it if it is heavy.

This is dangerous for the same reasons other email tauntings are dangerous.

Collection of Counterfeits

There are a number of people who have a collection of counterfeit money orders and cashier's checks displayed on their walls. These were obtained from Nigerian scammers who try to overpay for items and trick the victims into sending back the excess payment by bank transfer or Western Union.

This is dangerous because you have to give the scammer a real address and a real name. They may notice the same name and send something not so nice if they realize the same person is wasting their time over and over.

Scammer to Scammer

Collect fake cashier's checks from Nigerian scammers and re-send them to other scammers who want payment sent to Romania or Nigeria for the purchase of vehicles.

There are people who pretend to go along with the Nigerian scams in order to receive the counterfeit checks. They will then contact sellers of obviously fraudulent eBay Motor vehicle auctions. These fraudulent sellers offer an outside of eBay deal and the buyer says they must send a cashier's check because they have no Western Union office locally. The scammer then receives the fake cashier's check that was made by the first scammer. The second scammer does not remember what the original payment amount was and does not care. As long as they think they have received a big check they can steal, they are happy. The check will bounce when the second scammer tries to deposit it. If they cash it, the check is either refused because the bank calls to verify first or it is cashed and the person who cashed it is now on the bank's video cashing a counterfeit check.

This is also dangerous and by sending a counterfeit check you could be violating a number of laws simply by sending it through the mail.

I do not recommend doing any of these things. I cover them here because I know some people enjoy doing them, but they do not realize the risks. The best way to get even with a scammer is to turn them into the police.

CONCLUSION

There will always be scams where money changes hands. Even if eBay could put a notice at the top of every fraudulent auction saying

WARNING FRAUDULENT AUCTION,

someone would still bid on it and then complain when he was scammed.

I know you will pay attention to the next auction and watch for the obvious signs of a scam. Always check out the seller before placing a bid and look for indications their account has been hijacked. Check out the final pages of this book, I have packed them with free bonuses for you.

Also, please share what you have learned with others. The more people know about scams, the less effective the scams become.

Do you know about a scam I missed? Do you have more information on protection or spotting scams? Let me know and maybe I will include it in the next edition. support@ScamsAndScoundrels.com or reach me through Auction-Safety.org

APPENDIX
MORE INFORMATION

Keep Up to Date!
There are always new scams, or more accurately new twists on old scams. Visit our free website for the latest information or to report a bad user. When you file a complaint here, it will generate a custom report that tells you what you should do next and offer advice on how to possibly recover your money or goods:

www.Auction-Safety.Org

Protect Yourself From Spoof Websites
Download the free My Little Mole toolbar from

www.MyLittleMole.com

It will warn you if you visit a spoof PayPal, eBay, or many thousands of other fake or scam websites. It also has some very useful search features. You can also download the free PayPal toolbar. It does not offer the same extensive coverage that My Little Mole does, but it is a good backup, available from paypal.com

More Tools(THEY ARE FREE TOO!!)

I love free stuff and here are some great sites which are completely free:

www.Snipe-To-Win.com This website offers a free bid sniping service. Visit the site and download a free buide to Snipe Bidding.

www.TadpoleAuctionWatcher.com The Tadpole Auction Watcher is one of the most handy, useful, cool applications ever made. It monitors eBay for you and alerts you when things you like are posted for sale or watchs specific auctions you are interested in. Of course, it is also free. Go to the above site and download it now.

www.AuctionInquisitor.com Download the Auction Inquisitor Auction Analysis Tool here. It will warn you if it detects common signs of a fraudulent auction. Simply paste the auction number in the program and it will generate a safety report which warns you if it detects common signs of fraud.

PayPal
   Service Center 402-935-2050
   Only available during business hours and evenings.
   Caller must have phone number, email address, and last four digits from
   their credit card or bank account registered with PayPal.

Western Union
Western Union Fraud Investigations Department 1-800-634-1311
Let the customer service representative know you wish to report fraud
involving a Western Union money transfer.

Resources for Mail Fraud Complaints

U.S. Postal Inspection Service - online and mail in complaint forms are
available through
   http://www.usps.com/postalinspectors/
Find your local Postal Inspector Office
   http://www.usps.com/ncsc/locators/find-is.html

Internet Crime Complaint Center for the FBI
   http://www.ic3.gov/

FTC Federal Trade Commission
   http://www.ftc.gov/

National Fraud Information
   http://www.fraud.org/

Privacy Rights Clearing House
   http://www.privacyrights.org/

Identity Theft Resource Center
   http://www.idtheftcenter.org

Better Business Bureau
   http://www.bbb.org/

International links and other direct links can be found at
   http://portal.dont-bid-on-it.com

Find WHOIS registration information on websites
   http://whois.domaintools.com

SquareTrade
   http://www.squaretrade.com

Updates

eBay sometimes makes changes to their service so here are some of the latest changes that you should know about. Details about these changes are included with the *Don't Bid On It Book and System.*

Expanded seller protection from PayPal
Protection for any shipping address, not just a confirmed address
Unlimited annual coverage, not just $5,000 per year
Global coverage, extended to 190 countries around the world

Feedback Changes

1.Buyers will only be able to receive positive Feedback.
2.Positive repeat customer Feedback will count (up to 1 Feedback from the same buyer per week.)
3.Feedback more than 12-months old won't count towards your Feedback percentage. Other sites like yahoo and amazon have been doing this for years and it is we
4.When a buyer doesn't respond to the Unpaid Item (UPI) process the negative or neutral Feedback they have left for that transaction will be removed.
5.When a member is suspended, all their negative and neutral Feedback will be removed.
6.Buyers must wait 3 days before leaving negative or neutral Feedback for sellers with an established track record, to encourage communication.
7.All Feedback must be left within 60 days (compared to 90 days today) of listing end to encourage timely Feedback and discourage abuse. This is important because it changes the advice given in Don't Bid On It and Scams and Scoundrels. You now only have 60 firm days.
8.Buyers will be held more accountable when sellers report an unpaid item or commit other policy violations.

Wait, there are a lot more changes plus I explain how the affect you and what you need to know to continue trading safely on eBay. There were too many to list here so I have them on my website with the latest updates. You can find them
by going to the special bonus page
where you can also download your
bonus report. Look at the next page...

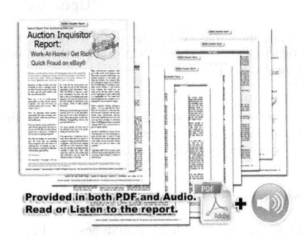

MORE SCAMS!

There are more scams I could not fit in this book!

I could not include everything I wanted to in this book so I prepared a special report series just for you! There are five reports and they are part of the eBay Mastery course. These exclusive reports are not available by themselves. The mastery course includes both the pdf and audio versions of these reports, an audio version of this book and an audio version of *eBay 102* (Dont' Bid On It).

Find out how you can get your copy at **http://Bonus.Dont*Bid*On*It*.com**

FREE: Snipe Bidding!

If you do not know what Snipe Bidding is, then you do not know how to bid on eBay!

Experienced bidders use a bidding technique called Snipe Bidding which gives them an advantage over regular bidders. Find out how this revolutionary bidding system works and how it can give you the same advantage. The report is free and it is not selling anything, it is actually giving more stuff away for free. Go to the below site and download your copy while it is still available.

www.Snipe-To-Win.com

www.ingramcontent.com/pod-product-compliance
Lightning Source LLC
Chambersburg PA
CBHW060154060326
40690CB00018B/4104